C000255647

PAUL BIF

Collected Poems

1987–2010

Hearing Eye

Published by Hearing Eye 2010

Hearing Eye
Box 1, 99 Torriano Avenue
London NW5 2RX, UK
email: books@hearingeye.org
www.hearingeye.org

ISBN: 1-905082-55-1

Second impression, Autumn 2010

ACKNOWLEDGEMENTS

SOME OF THESE POEMS FIRST APPEARED IN THE FOLLOWING PLACES:

The Guardian, The Independent, Daily Express, Morning Star, Liverpool Daily Post, Irish Post, Peace News, The Spectator, New Statesman, The Author, London Magazine, Outposts, Acumen, The Rialto, The SHOp, Orbis, The Interpreter's House, Poetry and Audience, The Wolf, Envoi, Poetry Nottingham, The Frogmore Papers, Spokes, The Echo Room, Scratch, Pennine Platform, Psychopoetica, Braquemard, Gargoyle, Brixton Poets, Tops, Shrike, Rising, The Eggbox, Ape, Trespass, South Bank Poetry, Aisle 16, Ravage, The Liberator, Baby Bubble, Still, Poetry Seen, Unexpected Item, Dial 174, Unpublished, Le Monstre, Poetry Street, The Delinquent, Krax, Poetry On The Buses, Poetry On The Internet, and were included in the anthologies: Velocity, In The Company Of Poets, Oral, Saltpetre, Reigning Cats and Dogs, Out From Beneath The Boot, Poems For The Retired Nihilist, Artefiction, The Real Survivors, In Dark Times, Well Versed, The Dead Good Poets Society,

and were broadcast on:
BBC Radio Merseyside, BBC Radio 4, BBC London Live, Resonance FM, Radio 100 Amsterdam, and were featured in films made by students of the London International Film School, by Ben Gregor, and by Omnia Films.

Printed and bound by Imprintdigital.net
Designed by Martin Parker at www.silbercow.co.uk

CONTENTS

Terrifying Ordeal

So Far So Bad

Rats Getting Close

Poems 2002–2003

Odd Behaviour

Willing to Change

Do Not Disturb

New Poems

TERRIFYING ORDEAL

KEEPING WATCH

There is a history of insanity
in that family going back three
generations and they watch each
other like hawks for signs.
They are over-controlled in that house
impulsive behaviour is non-existent.
I stayed there once and nobody
laughed shouted sang cried or
did anything emotional they just
watched – they watched each other
like hawks for signs and
one said as I was leaving,
"It's in our genes you know..."

79 KINGFIELD

There wasn't much room
in our house so I crashed
in Ma's room 'til I was ten...

Sometimes she'd get up and
piss in an orange bucket
Quite often she'd see something
and call out
I hated the night...

Occasionally the old man
would creep in, tip-toe
past my bed and give
her one, unaware I was
awake listening.
They were both in their fifties
I hated the night...

She became ill and
moaned with pain
throughout the night
getting up to take
pills walk about
and piss in the orange bucket.
The old man stopped coming...

When I was ten my
dad built an attic on
the roof and I got my own room
small though it was
the nights were peaceful,
I learnt to sleep...

PROBLEMS DESCRIBING A DEAD PERSON

The argument was about
whether or not LOVING FATHER
should be inscribed on his
tomb and it raged for three
days and three nights with
short breaks for food. Many
a violent word was spoken
and at one point Fred said
he'd smash the grave with
a hammer. It was finally
resolved by a sensitive
neighbour who came up
with an acceptable compromise
SADLY MISSED BY SOME.

CHRISTMAS IN BEDSIT LAND

Christmas is coming
and there's a violent maniac
in the attic.
He keeps threatening to
come down and give me a
good hiding because I have
lots of callers and he has none.
I've told the landlady but
she sez she can't evict him
until he actually gives me
the hiding.
He sez he's gonna do it
right after the Queen's speech
and I believe him...

CHEATING DEATH

No ambulance siren
No audience or crowd
No morbid doctor with
shocking diagnosis
No months of pain
and messing the bed
No operating theatres
or cream painted wards
just two hundred tranquillisers
and a room by the sea
Oh yes it's Hastings for me...

GETTING TO SEVENTY

I haven't got the skills
friends or family to take
me up to seventy.
I haven't got the will
qualifications or necessary
experience to take me
up to seventy.
I haven't got the health
stamina or special
relationship to take
me up to seventy.
I might make fifty though...

WAITING FOR MY MOTHER

Fifty-three and totally grey
wishing to avoid the
young mothers – was always
      last to arrive.
I could wait twenty minutes
and then, when the road was clear
in an old coat, looking tired
      and perhaps
      a little embarrassed
      she'd appear.
I was always pleased to
see her – well worth
waiting for was my old mum.

COUPLES

Couples are a nuisance
they're always waiting
for you to leave so they
can start mauling one another.
There's only me and this
fat kid with glasses left
in the village who haven't
got a girlfriend and he's
asked me to go on holiday;
everybody's watching us.

OUT WALKING WITH MY FATHER

That woman's got
cancer of the hand
it may spread
it may not.
That building's not safe
it's going to collapse
and kill people –
little children probably.
A man strangled
a woman in that
park last year.
That dog could
bite you and
give you rabies.
Watch a car
doesn't hit you
or you'll end up
with no legs.
Out walking with my father
the world became a terrifying place...

OBSESSIVE THINKER

He doesn't go to work
just lies on his bed
and thinks
He reads no books and
writes no letters
just lies on his bed
and thinks
In fact he has no hobbies
or interests except that
is to think
He doesn't drink in company
prefers to drink and think.
He eats TV dinners – they're
quick an' easy to prepare
which means more time
to think
He never goes to sleep at night
just lies there and thinks
And what does he think about?
Whether or not he's having a good time

WILL I BE ABLE TO DIE

Will I be able
to die
Do I have
what it takes
Do I have
the guts
Will I be able
to relax enough
when the time comes
– let go completely
or might I chicken
out at the last moment
and will the doctor
have to smother me with
a pillow – how humiliating...

LONER

He was so used to his own company
that whenever anyone
spoke to him – asked
him his name or how
he was feeling – assumed
for a moment he had just
been in a road accident and
they were trying to keep him alive...

SAD BASTARD

Wears shades to
hide the pain
health irrelevant
appearance unimportant
happiness not recalled
No-one likes a sad bastard...

Alone in a pub
not looking around
not interested
quite still
life's a chore
No-one likes a sad bastard...

Snivelling in a bedsit
eating beans from a can
ripping up suicide notes
watching a kids programme
No-one likes a sad bastard...

Shuffling through a park
having bitter thoughts
chucks stones at the ducks
shouts abuse at a squirrel
lies in the wet grass and cries
No-one wants a sad bastard...

Passes the Samaritans
on his way home
gives it two fingers
and starts to run
A sudden flash of courage
– he can do it,
this time it's for real
who'll miss a sad bastard...

STRANGERS ON A TUBE

He picked his nose
She laughed
He wiped it on her coat
She slapped his face
He head-butted her
I carried on reading Keats –
thank God for poems on the Underground...

THE MAN WHO COULDN'T CHANGE

He watched his sister change
many times during her breakdown
so equated it with madness
and like a dead tree – for
fifteen years forced himself
to stay, and be, exactly the
same; in case they should send
him to the asylum too.

ONLY THE APPALLING DIE OLD

Do you have a nasty
little plan to get
you through your
horrible span.

How many people
will you destroy
to bring about
your pride and joy.

And will you have
the cheek to say
there simply was
no other way...

BITTER OLD FART

I didn't smoke
and now I'm deaf...

didn't drink
now I'm incontinent...

didn't have late nights
now I'm senile...

didn't eat junk food
yet I can hardly see...

didn't take drugs
yet I ache all over...

didn't laze about
yet I'm stuck in this chair...

didn't get fat
now I've shrunk...

didn't take risks
now I stink the
place out...

didn't overspend
now I'm poor...

I never really enjoyed myself
like other people but they're
all dead, and I'm alone...

THE SHED

I watched the new tenants
pull down the old shed on Sunday afternoon
and remembered the day it was first
erected, some twenty years ago.
It took half an hour to dismantle
yet had taken the Gunnings two
sons, Francis and Arthur most of
an afternoon to build. Their parents
who were on holiday at the time
had been pestering them to put one
up for months, and I think it was
meant as a surprise. When they
had finished they began to argue
and then fight. I shouted
at them both to stop as they rolled around
the lawn exchanging blows and screaming
at one another, but they took no notice.
Then Arthur grabbed a hammer and walloped
Francis several times over the head with it
– he later died in hospital. The Gunnings
returned home the next day to discover they'd
gained a shed and lost a son...

BODY TALK

I hate my body
and it hates me
I fill it with tar
and tons of ale
it responds with
horrible pains
We have no respect
for one another
we give each other hell...

I exercise it rarely
and feed it some
awful shit it
retaliates with more
horrible pains
What a carry on...

Soon we'll part company
and the fighting will end
but not before it puts
me through agony for the
years I've mistreated it
horrible bloody thing...

REINCARNATION

Is this ladybird
Sir Oswald Mosley
Is this cockroach
Sir Stafford Cripps
Is this beetle
Pitt the younger
Is my cat Heydrich
'the hangman'
I'll boot its arse
just in case...

NERVOUS TWITCH

Can you imagine anything more unfashionable
than an uncontrollable nervous twitch like
shaking your head or blinking your eyes for
instance. I often wonder about twitches and
how disastrous it would be to develop one.
I sit in my executive chair and shudder at
the thought of shaking my head down at the
club or screwing up my face hideously at a
dinner party – I'd lose all my social status
in one twitch. I might even become an outcast
if it got bad enough – a laughing stock for
sure. Sometimes I stand in front of the mirror
do a few little twitches and then run to the
drinks cabinet and pour myself a large whisky.

FATHER-IN-LAW

He didn't like the mechanic
who wanted the daughter he
fancied but after a fight
gave her away. They moved
next door and now both men
enjoy a pint together on
Sundays, talk about sex and
work under the car...

VEGETARIAN

I wish I was a vegetarian
sometimes, then I could
boil a potato and eat it
with a stupid smile on my face...

ME TOO

Some of these poets
have big ideas especially
after they've had a few beers
– imagine they'll be read
in a hundred years...!

GETTING THROUGH

Struggling striving surviving
but for what?
So you can die
So you can say
you got through
but to who?
those fellow sufferers
merely getting through.
You're punishing yourself
for nothing and the dead
are laughing at you...

LOVE

Those who need love the least
get the most and those who
need it the most often get
none at all.

The happy get happier
while the sad get sadder
– cruel state of affairs...

LOVE AT FIRST SIGHT

Girl meets washing machine
Spin dryer, dishwasher, fridgedaire
three piece suite, colour telly
body guard, handyman entertainer
Sperm bank, back hander large garden
foreign holiday, chauffeur microwave
persian carpet, loft conversion
electrical appliance bit of jewellery
widow's pension...

BABIES AND BEARDS

Women must have kids
– try it at least once
as men do with beards.
But beards don't cause
wars poverty and unhappiness...

AFFECTION

Couldn't show it
Didn't know it
Thought it was
a diseased condition.
Such a shame
No-one to blame...

THE HAIRCUT

How are you?
Alright.
What'll it be?
The usual.
What's that?
Don't you remember?
No.
You just asked me how I was.
(PAUSE)
Don't you remember me?
No I'm afraid not.
Do you remember this lump
on the back of my neck?
Oh yes I remember that.
The usual is it?
Yes and make sure
the hair covers it...

STINKIN' PARTY

Flirting with an assortment of sheer rubbish
exchanging lines with smiling enthusiasts
thirsting for dialogue.
A hundred or so bloody good moods
crammed into a noisy little room.
Half dancing rotating heads scouting
for a spouse to spend half a century with.
Excited enough to wet your pants like a
dog that's been chained up for a week.
Burying one's liquor in the garden to
ensure drunkenness throughout.

Bell warns of new arrivals with fresh dialogue.
But why should I converse with these keen
sparkling hyped up shit-bags who've been
ignoring me on the underground all week.
Giving them the attention reserved for dying relatives
they'll not get a peep out of me.

Wish I was the gate-crasher who treads
dog muck into every carpet, nicks a few ornaments,
– fucks off early.

Those with style, superior lines and an
above average jig end up in a room fit
for pigs spending the remainder of the
night rolling round a cold floor
touching up several stone of unfamiliar
foul smelling flesh.

They take it to a bit of green
the next day, clutch its grubby
hand like they've known it for years –
make arrangements for a weekend by the sea.

Eighty per cent of accidents
occur in the home, why can't
we see a few at parties...

GOD WORKS IN MYSTERIOUS WAYS

Aberfan, Multiple Sclerosis
Spastics and the Somme
Bloody Mysterious...

Cancer, Culloden
Famine and President Botha
Weird...

Motorway pile-ups
Cot-deaths and Hiroshima
A trifle peculiar...

Schizophrenia, Zeebrugge
Thatcherism and Belsen
Damn strange...

Aids and Ulster
Strokes, Cardboard City
and of course the
human being

Is he worth an hour
on Sunday?
Surely not...

GIVE ME A BOY AT AN IMPRESSIONABLE AGE

I dance
like a Roman Catholic

Almost no movement...

I stare at women's breasts
like a Roman Catholic

Barely a glance...

I talk about sex
like a Roman Catholic

A couple of lines when I'm pissed...

I hug like a Roman Catholic
when seeing someone off on a journey
(Only)

I make love
like a Roman Catholic

In the dark ashamed...

I'm drinking myself to death

(and I'm not even a Roman Catholic)

PRIEST WITHOUT A HEAD

When I was a child
I used to dream a lot
of headless priests
coming towards me in
their silk vestments –
arms stretched out.
My dad told me seeing
the priest without a
head meant that I would
lose my faith as an adult.
Some years later our parish
priest lost his head in a car crash...

TRAGIC SMELL

The whisky
on your breath
smells horrible.
It smells of domestic
violence deprived children
and good friends lost forever.

The whisky
on your breath
is making me sick.
It smells of corruption
in low places the theft
of fifteen pounds a cheap
affair and losing at the races.

The smell of whisky on your breath
makes me quite depressed...

LOVED AND SLAUGHTERED

Better to have loved and lost
than never to have experienced rejection.

Better to have loved and lost
than never to have suffered
humiliation and pain.

Better to have loved and lost
than never to have felt
jealousy and hate.

Better to have loved and lost
than never to have known
such despair.

Better to have loved and lost
than never to have felt
like a total ass.

Better to have loved
and lost than never
to have swallowed
a bottle of pills.

Better to have loved
and lost than never
to have kept your
pride and dignity.

Better to have loved
and lost than never
to have lost at all...

WAKING UP

Last night I dreamt
I was a child again
playing by a stream.

Last night I dreamt
I was on holiday and
fell in love.

Last night I dreamt
it was my twenty-first
birthday and I was very
drunk.

This morning I awoke in
my hospital bed remembered
I was dying and cried..

THE UNKNOWN GLASS COLLECTOR

There was an old glass collector
in Maida Vale who often pestered
me whilst I drank my ale.
He boasted many friends –
I thought he must be sound
Yet he was dead four weeks
before his body was found...

NEUROSIS

Being tense a way of life
as happy as your phobias allow
A cripple without a wheelchair...

Frightened to live
frightened to die
Alcohol, fags – valium nearby...

No peace of mind
a conflict with self
Shrinks, bad dreams
Palpitations and dizzy spells...

Obsessional behaviour
the order of the day
A twitch here
a twitch there
touching this
touching that
Compulsive thoughts
you'd rather not have...

Only half living
in a kind of purgatory
with contorted face
and bleak outlook
sympathy from no-one
no chance of a cure...

ALTON'S AMENDMENT

Measles, the stick
exams and acne
bullying at the dentist
prefer to have my spine bust.

Unemployment or mundane tasks
broken hearts and shattered
dreams, accidents rape, worrying
to an ulcer, tranquillisers or
booze? break my spine instead.

Middle-aged failure,
depressed wasted debts,
boredom and balding.
Sooner have my head crushed.

Diseases, senility
operations and loneliness
mugged for tuppence.
No more praying
it's nearly over now
just some agonising pain
and the nightmare ends.

Hope no stinkin' couple
disturbs my sleep again...

JILTED

She said I was a bore
and took off with a stevedore
She said I was dull
and when I did talk
it was mostly bull
She said I was ineffective in bed
and suspected weird things
went on in my head
She said I lacked bite
and couldn't imagine me
winning a fight
She said I'd be no good
as a dad
– that all her kids would
turn out mad
She said we were an
incorrect match
and I was an incredibly
shitty catch...

SO MANY WAYS TO DIE

So obsessed with death
in all its forms – he
wanted to die not once,
but a thousand times –
trying every single cause
of death known to man.
How frustrating he thought
that a person could only
die of one ailment. However
he was comforted by the fact
there may be complications...

FALLING IN SHIT

A certain smile
or silly look
An accent or a laugh
some hackneyed phrase
or witty one liner
I'm falling in shit...

A piece of cabbage
between the teeth
A raincoat soaked through
tripping in the street
dropping an ice cream
nearly choking on a fishbone
I'm falling in shit...

A cut finger
some burnt sausages
An unusual gift
a thoughtful gesture
A birthmark, plaster
pattern on a jumper
I'm falling in shit...

Some angry exchanges
a button coming off a shirt
a sad tale
A bit of eccentricity
a minimum of defects
– possibly going places
I've fallen in shit...

WORK-SHY WRITER

You get lazy people
in any field, I write poems
instead of novels. You start
at nine and finish at half
past and have the rest of
the day to yourself – money's
crap though...

SMOKING IN BED

I always have a cigarette
last thing
I turn out the light
lie back and spark up
I love to smoke in bed...

Often I wake up
with my quilt on fire
or the ashtray over my head
There are holes in my
Pillow and sheets
but I love to smoke
in bed...

One day the whole
house will go up
and there are kiddies
in the flat above
But I don't give
a monkey's
I love to smoke
in bed...

TERRIFYING ORDEAL

Sex is smelly
sex is bad
messy and 'orrible
not in my pad...

Hate the word
loathe the effort
diseases brats
and raised blood pressure...

Clumsily in the dark
we fiddle about
a pathetic attempt at affection
about as relaxing as having a tooth pulled...

Embarrassing pointless
overrated nonsense.
A time consuming
unhygienic farce
enjoyed by shit-heads...

A competitive complicated
recurring nuisance
an absurd form of communication
favoured by pea brains...

Wipe my arse
and I'll wipe yours
but no more please
nothing about you turns
me on except the cancer-
growth I suspect blossoms
in your breast...

FEMINIST

If I were a feminist
I should prefer a
bible-thumping misogynist
to a liberated male
who changes one in
ten nappies and lets
me go to my night-class
on Thursdays...

AIM LOW SCORE HIGH

Whilst trying
to emulate Jesus Christ
I lost all my friends
and got my head kicked
in four times.
My mate on the other hand
who was inspired by King
Herod in his early teens
seems to be having a ball
of a time – everybody loves him.
I might have a crack at Bonaparte
when I leave hospital...

PESTERING THE DOCTOR

I rang my doctor this morning
and asked him if wearing tight
jeans would aggravate my sciatica.
He told me he had people dying
of cancer in his surgery and hung up.
So I rang him back and asked would
it be safe to re-heat a steak 'n' kidney
pie from yesterday...

DATING

I always give a heil Hitler salute
on my first date and rant on about
badger baiting.
I never show my good side,
they always bugger off.

Sometimes I smack myself in the face,
refuse to buy a round, or talk about
life in a mental hospital.
I never show my good side,
they always bugger off.

But usually I just get steaming drunk
and talk of human scum – this one never
fails to alienate and send them on the run...

THOUGHT FOR THE DAY

I wish for once the
day would not begin
the night is not long
enough – it seems no time
at all and the birds start
their bloody twittering and
we're off again...

BAD BACK

Can't bend
Can't lift
Can't slouch
Unsexy uncool
Can't sit on a
Bleedin' stool
Girls hate a bad back...

Doesn't show on X-ray
Difficult to prove
Work-shy dole cheat
Malingering fraud
The State hate a bad back...

Difficult to treat
Impossible to cure.
A baffling mystery
A nuisance an' a bore
Doctor's hate a bad back...

CHEER UP

Sometimes when I'm
feeling a bit low
I imagine I'm out
walking in the
New Forest, about
to tread on an adder.

TWO SHORT LOVE POEMS

LAZY

How can I fall in love
I can't even muster the
energy to clean out the toilet...

BETTER

Better to have loved and lost
than to have lived in a caravan...

WANKING

The best value for
money I know
An unstressful private
business hurting no other.

Anytime, anywhere
this simple act can
be enjoyed by young
and old alike.

Imagination ensures
a good time
Magazines videos
and binoculars
for the less inspired.

The oldest thrill
known to man
Enjoyed by Moses
written about by
the apostles.

Five minutes a day
keeps frustration
at bay
A bit of handwork
a box of tissues
and you're away.

Wanking!
for the way you live
your life today...

ALARM CALL

When I was eighteen
still living at home
I was awoken each morning
by the screams of a then
undiagnosed schizophrenic.
She'd run upstairs bang
on my door and ask me
what I wanted for my birthday.
Sometimes she'd ask me when
I thought I might die and go
away laughing.
My sister now lives on her own by the sea
and I have an alarm clock...

MAD COW

She's a mad cow
suffering from mad cow disease
and the mad cow is going to die
because there's no cure – so die
cow die, die you mad cow...

IAN BOTHAM'S UNDERPANTS

Stylish career women
spin round in minis
and have nicer legs than nurses...

Hard and cold
like their men tough, but sane
Never progressing from the wendy-house
only looks keep them out the gutter...

Spirited face-slappers
G-strings with spending power
disguising their common origins
Seducing Alsatian dogs...

Normally blonde, quite often
stupid, always Tory.
Union Jacks and make-up
Prawn cocktails in Spain...

Secretly loathing the tattooed
muscles they cuddle each night
too thick to be lesbian
prefer watching Cave-men scrap...

Haters of the Wimp
intolerant of the Weirdo
inspired by the crook
Prepared to fight tooth and nail
for a pair of Botham's undies.

SCRATCHED CAR

Before terminating our friendship
he gave me a lecture.
I had to listen
he held the moral high ground
I scratched his car you see;
used my keys and went right
around forming a circle almost.
I offered him a pair of scissors
and told him to cut the arm of
my new leather jacket but he
declined and continued with
his lecture – verbal psychopath...

MEN AND MOTHERS

Fussing cuddling
ironing my short pants
I can handle this jungle
Cos mum's about...

And when I get older
and mummy is dead
I'll find a substitute
to pat my head...

She'll not be like mum
but will have a nice bum
she'll fail all mum's tests
but will have nice breasts...

If she's disloyal, unlike Ma'mar
I'll get stinking in my local bar.
Then back home I'll throw a fit,
and knock the wench about a bit...

ME OR THEM

Is it me
or is it them
Is it me
or is it them
Is it me
or is it them
Why do I live
on my own
Is it me
or is it them...

FOR TED HUGHES

The birds are migrating
– who gives a fuck ...

CONVERSATION

Fact
joke
interruption
lie
silence
fact
pause
wind up
insult
rubbish
half truth
exaggeration
mug's game

NEVER TIRING

I wish I could
live a hundred times
in a hundred different places
as a hundred different people
a hundred years a piece ...

SHOULD HAVE GUESSED

I always wondered
about you.
I should have guessed
really it was obvious.
Even at school I suppose
the signs were there,
and then afterwards when
you avoided everyone,
Why didn't I realise
you were in the Knights
of St Columba...

SLEEPING AROUND

Sleeping around
Sleeping around
What is all this
Sleeping around

Sleeping around
Sleeping around
Where is all this
Sleeping around

Sleeping around
Sleeping around
Why is there all this
Sleeping around

Sleeping around
Sleeping around
Who's doing all this
Sleeping around...

JUST HAD TO KNOW

Obsessed with the idea of an afterlife
climbed out onto his tenth floor balcony
and shouted 'In ten seconds I'll know
the answer to the question we've all
wondered about since time began.' But
as he went to jump caught his foot
in the rail and was left dangling
over the edge for half an hour,
eventually dropping into a large
blanket which the laughing crowd
held out...

EYEWITNESS

Yesterday I witnessed
something quite strange.
My next door neighbour
a Jehovah's witness stole
a pint of milk from my
doorstep and drank it in
his garden laughing...

DISTURBED

A fire rages in my mind
– the inescapable torture
of an unresolved unforgiving
past that returns to haunt me.
Time does not and cannot heal
this festering wound which does
not abate and only a death, without
an afterlife to still remember will
kill this mortal flame of torment...

ILL AT EASE

I've always felt
uncomfortable on this planet
never quite at ease
forever looking over my shoulder
or checking my pulse
I don't know what it is
really but I just can't
get comfortable...

NOT CELEBRATING THE NEW DECADE

Didn't care to celebrate
maybe falling down the stairs
electrocuting myself losing
one or both parents getting
hit by a car – having my first operation
No hugs for me at twelve o'clock
I sat in a dark room biting my nails...

Didn't care to celebrate my
relationship ending badly
my hair falling out getting
into debt some form of mental
illness my first suicide attempt
another world war
No hugs for me at twelve o'clock
I sat in a dark room shaking
uncontrollably...

Didn't care to celebrate
losing my job getting
butted in a bar ominous pains
in my left arm and not prepared
to revel in future misfortunes
sat chain smoking in a dark room
No hugs for me at twelve o'clock...

TO ME

He did this to me
to me to me
he did it to me
He hit me – me me
he hit me

She was rude to me
to me – was rude to me
She jilted me
Me jilted me

He stole off me
Me me he stole
off me

I liked him until
I discovered he
didn't like me
– me me he didn't
like me

They said bad things
about me about me
no-one else me me
Said bad things about me

I hung myself
Me me I hung me...

TALKING IN BOXES

A man in a box
told me to watch my step.
A man in a box
told me to stop pissing around.
A man in a box
told me to shut my face.
A man in a box
told me to get it sorted.
A man in a box
told me I was a dead cert
for the big fire.
I went to confession yesterday...

EARLY IMPRESSIONS

Dad locked in
a room won't come out
sound of him laughing
wants to join a religious order.
Sister in another room
not talking to anyone
won't answer pretending
to read a book.
The doctor calls shouts
at her but she carries on
not reading.
Ambulance arrives takes
her away she leaves the book
by the side of the chair but
I am frightened to look at it...

THE GREAT HUMAN FARCE

I love you
I hate your guts
You're so kind
You're a cruel bastard
Shall we start a family
I'm having custody of the kids
You're so exciting
You're no fun anymore
Will you make love to me
Don't even touch me
I want to be with you
I've found somebody else
I really care about you
Drop dead!...

STRIVING FOR IMPERFECTION

Teach me to play the
game of life with all
its twisted rules.
Teach me positive thinking
that great human lie we
deceive ourselves with
in order to cope.
Help me to learn the
lie so I can survive too...

DIFFERENT KIND OF FATHER

My dad wanted
to be a priest
and my mum wanted
to be a house wife
and they fought like
cat and dog.
My dad called it
a pseudo marriage
– a con.
My mum called it
a disgrace.
They broke each other's
hearts and ours too
we buried them together...

STONE THROWING

Odd business that
throwing stones at one another
with intent to cause injury.
We don't do it any more of course.
There are more subtle ways of
hurting people.
I must have been thirteen
when I threw my last stone
in anger – I think I missed him...

PAUL

Remember how nice
it was to first be
called by your name
to hear it said,
especially by a friend.
Remember how nice it
was to first hear your
name – your own special
name and how important
you felt...

WIND UP

I was invited to dinner
by the vicar last week,
duck was mentioned.
I arrived on time with
a bottle of wine but he
did not answer the door.
I thought I saw the curtain move...

MY DOCTOR

I'm quite sweet on my doctor.
I gave her my book and invited
her to my reading.
(Needless to say, she didn't show up).
She has my medical records.
Why would she be interested in a
fat alcoholic predisposed to psychotic episodes?

PATRIOTIC WHITE YOUTH

Tattoos and flash wheels
nice little earners and thuggery
dodgy deals and racism
Cockneys make me sick.

Uncreative Unimaginative
money makes it tick
fancy clobber tedious slang
Cockneys make me sick.

Anti-trade unions subservient girlfriends
Individualistic – a mind of its own
except on the football terraces
Cockneys make me sick.

Loud mouthed show-offs won't be
ruled by Socialism, the cripple
beggar creed of Northern losers
Wheelchair politics is not for them
suntans and cash cards
Cockneys make me sick.

Big dicks and doing bird
keeping fit in case there's a war
bracelets medallions knives out
at the disco.

Oh! Come back stuka's all is forgiven
V2s and doodle-bugs do your stuff
rip the heart out this Capitalist monster
street by street like forty years ago.
Return and break their spirit once more
Cos cockneys make me sick.

DEATH

Death is a Socialist
he comes to us all
the rich the smug
the mad and the small...

The reaper's a lefty
a decent sort
he doesn't take
Barclaycard
he shits on us all...

He mocks our plans
causes much pain
arrives unannounced
in horrible forms...

Yet for all his faults
he ends suffering
for many and sorts out
the smart arses
once and for all...
I take my hat off to him,
death the greatest leveller
for sure...

THE SECRET CRIER

The old man wept
privately making
sure the windows
were closed and
mortise lock was
on the front door.
He had been caught
crying once before
in the trenches on
the Somme and had
been threatened
with a .38 revolver.

HORRIBLE THOUGHT

As I sat talking to the girl I loved
I noticed an axe on the fire-hearth
and a most unpleasant thought flashed
through my mind. It made me feel ashamed
guilty and rather horrible. I turned my
chair round so as not to see the axe but
it remained in my mind and I felt even
worse even more guilty that the axe had
such an effect on me it had caused me
to move my chair so I moved it back again.
'What's with all the chair movements', asked
my girlfriend. 'It's the axe isn't it?
I'll go and put it in the kitchen – out of
sight out of mind'.

NO SECONDS NO AFTERS

Oh cowardly humans
other animals can
accept death why can't
you. They don't go running
to church every five minutes
to listen to the deranged
prattle of some neurotic
vicar with a grotesque fear
of death. Just because you
can count to a hundred, write
the odd letter and still picture
your dead grandparents doesn't
mean you deserve to live forever.
Three score years and ten – say
it, say it instead of a prayer
and hold your head up high with
the other animals...

C2 H5 OH

One or two
I can't do
Three or Four
leads to more
Five or Six
I'm in a fix
Seven or Eight
lose a mate
Nine or Ten
never again
Anything over
nut-house in Dover...

HYPOCRITE

She said men are horrible –
they're sick they're violent
they start wars they kill easily
they're rough bullying domineering
tyrants, macho swines.
I agreed with her and said imagine
fancying one – how much sicker that would be
She slapped my face and left – collaborator...

MIRROR

Mirror Mirror
on the wall
why must I wear
this horrible colostomy bag...

Mirror Mirror
on the wall
explain the acne
on my face...

Mirror Mirror
on the wall
why the harelip
club foot and pissin' wheelchair...

EXPOSED

Trapped by his
semi-confessional
writings; was forced
into a role which
eventually killed him.
And for what? a few
miserable publications...

BRILLIANT STUDENT

Excelled in all subjects
a great sportsman
wonderful sense of humour
fell off a cliff...

Active in everything
lived life to the full
a generous nature
stabbed to death
at a disco...

A great guy
with a great future
cheerful and optimistic
head crushed in
a car crash...

Full of ideas
always dashing about
popular with the ladies
fell onto a javelin...

A kind heart
and sense of fairness
always fun to be with
inhaled his own vomit...

MAN TO MAN

She said she was getting
heavy phone calls and
wanted to borrow a man's
voice for the answer machine.
I volunteered immediately
but she said I'd be no good
on account of my stutter.

G.B.H.

I've pushed you off buildings
into trains and spikes
I've removed bits from
walls imagining your eyes
I've slashed pillows and
curtains butted doors
and shattered glass
I've done all this and more
Yet I still see you laughing
in a Glasgow bar...

THE LAVATORY ATTENDANT

I go to work
at my own convenience
angry and demoralised
sit on a stool
and dream of nice places...

In they trickle
coughing spitting
splashing about
I take out a book
but it doesn't help...

The smell is awful
the clients surly
can't bear to eat
my sandwich.
If only I'd passed
an exam or two
this job is hell...

There's sick on the floor
and a couple are screwing
in a cubicle I should really
say something but what's
the point.
This isn't a job it's
an insult...

5.30 the shitting
and pissing is over
time to lock up.
My clothes stink
and I just want to
get drunk...

UNHAPPY HOUR

I enter alone it is a
large pub and I go through
the nightly ritual of looking
in every room even though I
know I will recognise no one
the rest of the pub know this
too but I look anyway. Occasionally
I do see a familiar face but it
ignores me because it is frightened
of my loneliness so I pretend I
have forgotten those few lines
spoken when he or she was feeling
generous and skulk off to a quiet
corner thinking to myself it's
about time I left London...

NATURE POEM

This morning,
I observed from my bedroom window
two squirrels chasing each other –
from tree to tree they leapt but
it wasn't for my entertainment.
They had had a furious row which
had erupted into violence.
I suspect a woman may have been involved...

FIREMEN

Big fat sons of Satan
clumsy psychopaths
never on time...

Pathological liars
so full of hate
not a bit of compassion
never far from trouble...

Absolute cowards
obsessed with water
noisy buffoons
shouting about nothing...

Bone-idle incompetents
children in uniform
can start nothing
can only put things out...

The most corrupt
profession in the world
A job for sneaky
little shits and
greedy egomaniacs...

THE LONELY RASPBERRY BLOWER

All on my own except
for a phone.
I ring at cheap rate
to unleash my hate.
It's a form of art
a telephone fart.
It gives them a fright
in the middle of the night.
When I feel mean
I'm especially obscene.
I go on till I yawn
quite often dawn.
Then I make a cup of tea
and wonder if they think
it's me...

GAMES WITH GRANMA

Sometimes when my Gran
was sleeping I would have
fun tying her shoelaces
together or placing objects
on her head. One time I removed
her left eye with a bayonet...

HURRY UP AND DIE

I wish more people
I know would die
I like a good funeral
and seldom cry.

How long must I
wait for them to die
I like a good drink and
a piece of pie.

BEST SELLER

Poetry doesn't normally sell,
but mine might because I intend
to embark on a series of bizarre
motiveless murders on and around
Hampstead Heath. Poetry doesn't
normally sell, but mine might...

SUDDEN REALISATION

And then it occurred to him
maybe he hadn't lived at all

and was chuffed...

SO FAR SO BAD

WINTER OF '63

It snows for the first
time. My sister buys a trunk
for college and my father
gives her a black eye as
a leaving present – the
life experience has begun...

SECTIONED

They stand around me in
a big circle – arms folded
faces expressionless. I try
to explain that I'm not mad
and it's all a big mistake.
I plead my case strongly –
passionately as if my life
depended on it; and just
when I think I've won them
over – convinced them I'm
sane – this big black guy
appears from nowhere and
jabs me in the bum with a needle...

DEATH ON THE ROADS

I hate it when death
passes me by suddenly
in the shape of a red
transit van. A few seconds
later and I may have been
tossed into the air – waking
to the voice of a policeman
asking the crowd of morbid
onlookers did they see
what happened...

WHEN DID YOU LAST SEE YOUR FATHER?

Where's your father Paul?
down south miss
What's he doing there?
teaching miss
Why doesn't he teach
up here?
He likes the climate miss
When's he coming back?
Don't know miss
Why isn't he with
his family?
He can't stand us miss
Is that why you shake
your head?
Don't know miss
Alright sit down.

THE ROCK SHOP

We were always making
fun at the man in the
Rock shop. Once he got
very angry and began
throwing his stock at
us – rare stones of
varying colours whizzed
past our ears and my friend
was hit in the face with a
piece of malachite. The police
took him away and his shop
closed down. Some weeks later
he killed himself by swallowing
some pulverised granite.

CHEST PAINS AT 3AM

There goes another speeding ambulance
without its siren on – a heart attack
case – they don't like to cause them
undue stress. But they cause me stress.
I imagine the poor sod lying on a settee
gasping for breath and chewing an aspirin
his frantic wife and kids looking on –
how much easier to die on your own.
I wonder when it will be my turn,
and ring an ambulance to see how
long it takes to arrive – they are
not amused...

MILLENNIUM

It's weird seeing '2000' on things
because I, like some other people,
think the world's going to end –
computers going down, plane crashes...
I wouldn't mind, actually
I'll be forty, and I've got my book out
but my nephew's gutted –
he'll only be sixteen
and he wants a football career...

SIMPLY EVERYONE'S STOPPING
SMOKING CIGARETTES

The butcher's stopped
The dentist's cut down
The priest's switched
to charoots
The fishmonger's on
a pipe and the chemist
is taking snuff – simply
everyone's stopping smoking cigarettes
since the doctor had a heart attack...

WASTE OF TIME

First of all
you search for one.
Then you find you
like them but don't
fancy them.
You fancy them
but don't like them.
You fancy and like
them but they only
like you.
You fancy and like
them but they only
fancy you.
You fancy and like
them and they fancy
and like you – you
both fall in love
and in one to five
years one of you
fancies someone else
and it all ends sour...

SIX O'CLOCK

You make me feel like
a sick pervert – a disturbed
sadist, every time you leave
the room when I turn on the
news, because you don't watch
it and it's so bad...

TEACHERS ARE OVERPAID

Third-rate psychologists
substandard encyclopaedias
second-class citizens
grossly overpaid...

Verbal bullies
too cowardly for the police
talentless, unoriginal –
certificates to prove it.
Societies' outcasts
forced back to school...

Unenthusiastic, uninspiring
crashing bores with
a mental problem
so uninteresting as to
need a weapon.
Keep this poison
away from children...

Frustrated failures
enemies of the individual
punishers of creative thought
character assassins
receiving more than road sweepers...

Congenital idiots
award the most unworthy
penalise that which
they don't understand.
Is it any wonder they
occasionally get a kicking?

ON LOSING A MOTHER AT SIXTEEN

A bad age to lose a mother say some
psychologists – neither a boy nor
a man – a mere fledgling leaving
the nest. I was devastated – felt
lost, deserted even betrayed and
found it difficult to relate to
women for a long time after. I
wondered how I would fill all the
years of a life without her; although
as with my father's death some years
later it did give me a new sense of
freedom which I felt slightly guilty
about, but I don't think I could have
lazed around on the dole had she lived.
Like many immigrants she was obsessed
with her children's education and
sadly lived just long enough to learn
I'd failed most of my 'O' Levels.

STRANGLED BY A NEIGHBOUR

No chance to go dancing
No chance to go courting
No chance to have children
Oh to be slain at nine...

No chance to go travelling
No chance to go boozing
No chance to choose careers
Oh to be slain at nine...

No chance to have memories
No chance to have achievements
No chance to make friendships
Oh to be slain at nine...

No chance to grow older
No chance to grow wiser
No chance to be contented
Oh to be slain at nine...

HAVING YOUR PHOTOGRAPH
TAKEN IN LONDON

When someone produces a camera
and takes a photograph in a
London public place I normally
look annoyed and turn away
hoping they'll think I'm a
terrorist, undiscovered
murderer or prisoner on the
run. I have never smashed a
camera though, I wouldn't
take the role that far...

ENGAGED

The operator
has checked the line
and tells me there's
an interesting conversation
in progress.
I didn't think he had
it in him...

FINAL RESULTS

ABRAHAMS   63 – Bowel Cancer

BAYLISS   48 – Motor Neurone disease

BIRTILL   55 – Heart attack

BYRNE   40 – Suicide

CAMPBELL   86 – Cancer of the stomach

CREWDSEN   66 – Killed on a pedestrian crossing

DODD   29 – Heart attack

DUNCAN   68 – Lung cancer

EARWAKER   71 – Peritonitis

FITZGERALD   38 – Car crash

GILLIN   89 – Old age

HEATH   64 – Lung cancer

HERON   39 – Brain Haemorrhage

JOHNSON   93 – Old age

KENNY   19 – Murdered

KINSELLA   35 – AIDS

LARGE   60 – Pneumonia

LEE   42 – Chokes to death

LYNESS B   67 – Leukaemia

LYNESS J   81 – Stroke

MARRAY   73 – Heart attack

MURRY   43 – Brain Tumour

McQUAID   79 – Electrocuted

RASMUSSEN   71 – Heart attack

RYAN   74 – Fractured skull from fall

THOMAS A   87 – Killed in a fire

THOMAS F   60 – Heart attack

TRAYNOR   65 – Stroke

TURTLE   58 – High blood pressure

VENTREE   74 – Heart attack

WEDGWOOD   80 – Cancer of the throat

WELSH   70 – Cancer of the prostate

Good riddance to bad rubbish...

ONSET OF MADNESS

One day my sister
quite suddenly, without warning
went mad.
I remember I was in the garden
at the time playing with a friend
when I heard this awful scream.
I thought someone had had an
accident and froze. But then
came the sound of laughter
followed by more screams
and then shouting from my father.
'What's happening in there' asked
my friend I said I didn't know.
Then suddenly the kitchen door
flung open and my sister ran into
the garden naked screaming at the
top of her voice with my father
chasing after her. He told me to
dial 999 and ask for an ambulance,
my friend left...

PUB COLLECTION

They came round
again tonight with
their death-defying tins
collecting for bee-stings
to the throat violent
murder falling off
mountains getting
struck by lightning
fires and gas explosions
and I said:

"You can die of cancer too"...

TO NO LONGER BE ME

I don't want to lose me
I've grown used to me,
me is all I know.
I don't wish to lose
all my knowledge, memories
experiences, even my neurosis.
I know of no other existence
except being me. I can handle
saying good-bye to others,
but not me – we've shared so much...

CRUEL TO BE KIND

There was a man
who lived on his own
who behaved in a way
that no one should
ever love him – ignored
the game and social graces
and didn't break a single heart...

LIFE GOES ON

I dislike people
because they're
always getting
over things.
With such ease
they carry on
because they say
life must go on
but must it?
and is this really
the case or are they
just insensitive
miserable little
earthlings with
not much feeling
at all...

LOOSE CHANGE

Who would have the loose change
on my sideboard if I died today?
Would it be shared amongst my
family – given to my nephew for
pocket money – or put towards my
funeral expenses? Who would have
the loose change on my sideboard
if I died today?

OH GOD

Human beings are
confused little children
who know nothing about
anything. They don't even
know if they'll wake up
tomorrow and see another day.
They get absorbed in money,
politics and careers of every
sort – all diversions from the
truth – temporary refuge from
the terrible, unpalatable, unavoidable
truth – that they are dying, slowly
but surely each sombre day, hooray!

SO FAR SO BAD

How come I've ended
up like this
lying in my
own piss.
With no partner
or job – a
fifteen stone slob.
Each day as empty
as the last, no
future or present
only the past...

IMAGINE

Imagine if the only
way of dying was to
be kicked to death.
There would be thousands
of kickings every minute.
Every time you went out
to buy a newspaper you'd
see someone being kicked
to death; and you'd always
be wondering just when and
where and by whom you were
going to get your fatal kicking...

BARGAIN

My next door neighbour – strange woman,
smoked eighty Kensitas a day and collected
the coupons feverishly. I've saved enough
to buy a clock she said after having a lung
removed – I've just got a toaster she said
as her right leg came off. Will you collect
my portable television, she asked me as she
lay in hospital having had her third stroke
and a few years later as she lay dying what
seemed to upset her most was that she was
only ten points off a gorgeous mahogany coffin.

I DON'T THINK SO

Was the poem
good enough though?
Was it worth tapping
her on the shoulder
for the third time
to borrow her pen
again?

COUCH POTATO

Bet there's no-one
down the local I know
and the tickets for
that concert are all gone...

Bet that new restaurant's
a bleedin' rip off and that
night class is over-subscribed...

Bet there's a crush at
the football match and
they're not saying much
at that meeting...

Bet I wouldn't click
if I went to that club
and that party's a
false address

May as well just lie here
        and watch TV...

DEVASTATED

Yesterday I spent three
hours making a stew and
then dropped it on the
carpet. I was so upset
I rang the Police they
told me not to be so
stupid and asked me if
I lived on my own.

DEAD ERNEST

Ernest Hemingway
wasn't gay
but blew his brains out
anyway...

THE LEAST POPULAR ART FORM

Seventy per cent of poetry
is utter crap
meaningless nonsense
tedious dung
written by bores with nothing
to say who disguise the fact
in clever word play.
The vast majority of it
is fraudulent wanking and
should be thrown in the dustbin.
One shouldn't waste one's time
even looking at it, never mind
reading it and only a fool with
time on his hands attempts to
decipher it...

DEPRESSION

A great black hollow
which needs no feeding
it has no appetite
which hates the dawn
and longs for night
which needs no company
and gets none either
which does not work
just lies there still.

BIG LET DOWN

When I was a boy I would visit
my local library each Saturday
and borrow books about the lives
of famous people. Then I'd sit
and wonder what great, exciting
adventures lay before me. Now
I'm an old man and as my life
draws to a close I realise it's
all been a big let down. No leading
my armies into battle. No great
speeches in parliament. No Oscars,
Nobel prizes or travelling to exotic
places – not even an illicit love affair.
Just recently I've taken to borrowing
those same books again, but instead of
reading them I take them home and deface them.

PSYCHOLOGICAL GAMES

He doesn't care for monopoly
nor is he interested in chess.
He won't play cards or scrabble
but he does like power games and
will play them if you let him...

ENEMIES

I sometimes wonder what it would
be like to sit in a room full of
all the people who dislike me –
yet don't know each other – would
their common loathing of myself
unite them? Are they similar types
perhaps? Would they all get along?
And would I survive the experience?

LIFE'S NOT SHORT ENOUGH

Imagine if the lifespan
was only twelve – what
nicer people you and me
and how much simpler life
would be.

RESULT!

I've got a new girlfriend
who just happens to be my
doctor, and she wants to
see me again – she said
come back in a month's time.

POEM

Delivering the light of
madness, only to be snatched
away by the changeable
movements of the night – the
forgotten hero the moon watches
curiously and absorbs the chaos
of the moment...

LOST

You were miserable,
you said unhappy because
you were alone, inadequate
with no partner – not a unit.
Yet you painted pictures –
beautiful pictures of beautiful
cats. Now you have a man and are
happy? But paint pictures of tall
buildings and machinery or worse
don't paint at all.

...BASTARDS, NOT YUPPIES

A disease from the Home Counties
with money to spend
ambitious, competitive
striving little bleeders
Out to make good in their chosen fields
making London a shit place to be
Bastards...

High spirits and barbecues
parachute jumps for Cancer Research
Jogging in the Marathon
giving blood after a game of squash
Bastards...

Stinking lovers of life
buying up tree houses
on Hampstead Heath
Happy letters to Mummy and Daddy
admirers of Geldof and Waite
contempt for mining Arthur
Bastards...

Jeffrey Archer on the tube
night classes in French
travelling around Europe
with an old school pal
Independent as fuck
Bastards...

Wonderfully exciting
vibrant personalities
generating warmth and happiness
wherever they are
such fun to be with
when the bubbly flows
Bastards...

Accident! Did you see?
one of them got killed
crossing Baker Street
the other day
around 1:35
Nice one Lord...

POSITIVE THINKING

The muck used to cope with
life's continuous programme
of disasters – a pick-you-
up of self-deceit that grows
more cunning as the calamities
get more desperate.

SOLDIER IN THE SOIL

One summer I helped my dad dig
up the garden and found a beautiful
toy soldier buried in the soil.
It had obviously been there a long
time and none of us could make out
what army he belonged to. So my
father suggested we take it round
to Mister Dargy, an embittered old
army officer from World War One.
He wasn't very happy about being
disturbed but examined the soldier
closely and then roared 'I know who
this fellow is – he's a damned yellow
belly, a conscientious objector' and
bit its head off – I cried all the
way home.

JOE'S CAFE

There's bits of egg on
my liver because he only
uses one frying pan. There
are peas in my beans –
he couldn't care less
his place is a mess.
The fella opposite picks
his nose, the fella behind
coughs and splutters –
everyone stares at each
other's food. The tables
are filthy and there's
a bit of dog-dirt near
the door – think I'll
skip dessert.

HIGH PRICE

I only wanted a shag,
now I'm married with
three kids – working
all the hours God sends
and her mother stays most
weekends – wish I'd had
a wank instead...

MISANTHROPIST

He soon realised there
was no advice to be given
and no-one to respect and
without anything original
to offer became a hermit –
the alternative being a
liar or a cheat.

BEING FAT WITH MY CAT

I don't mind being fat
when I'm at home with my cat.
But when I go out I always feel stout.
People laugh and people stare.
But I don't care, because I don't
mind being fat when I'm at home
with my cat.

THE AGNOSTIC PRAYS

He never makes
the sign of the cross
or gets down on his
hands and knees.
He never prays
to a specialist saint
but he prays all the same,
and sometimes he wonders
whether his unconventional
prayers are ever answered
and by whom.

TWISTED

He was nice to me
when his girlfriend
was horrible to me
and was horrible to
me when his girlfriend
started to like me yet
I didn't like either
but was polite to both...

LONDON BARS

You never meet anyone
in a London bar, anyone
you know that is. London
bars are full of strangers –
lone rangers out on their
own or in pairs of two, they
won't talk to you.

You'll never make friends
in a London bar, even if you
travel far. They're unfriendly
places full of unknown faces
you never meet anyone in a
London bar...

DEATH

Total shutdown
an eternal state
of nothingness
a restless spirit
an awful dream
another life
a burning fire
      I'm scared...

DRAMA SCHOOL

When we're young we
train to be actors
and play all kinds
of roles. When we are
older and leave our
acting is better, even
good and sometimes if
we're lucky we get the
parts we want...

CALL FOR SOCKS AND UNDERPANTS

Socks and underpants
socks and underpants
We need socks and underpants
Men's Hostel Old Kent Road
      ...NO TIME WASTERS...

VIOLENCE AND CELIBACY

Men without women
glare at you in bars
don't wash or shave
sing or smile and
thump you at the
drop of a hat...

C OF E UPBRINGING

God mentioned once
Sunday school twice
lose virginity at ten
rock n' roll in teens
plenty of sex
drugs galore
horoscopes
I-Ching
palm readings
and witchcraft
hippy books
eastern mysticism
existentialist arsehole.
No respect
no guilt
no idea
totally confused –
divorced with kid
called Zoe at 25
and no better than
the wild beasts of
the jungle
C of E upbringing...

NO THANKS

Pendulous melons
and open wounds
that smell of fish
is not my dish...

CHANGES

I'm always wondering where
to move to – where I would
be happiest – city, country,
seaside. But really I would
like to move back to my childhood
to see the sky again for the
first time – the sun the stars
the snow – to climb trees and
run in the long grass. Then it
wouldn't matter where I was
because childhood is beautiful
anywhere...

PIGS AND SEX

Most people are ugly
and there's too much
sex about anyway – so
abstain you ugly fuckers
and leave sex to the good
lookers.

NEIGHBOURS

Neighbours
    lie
Neighbours
    spy
Neighbours
    die
        bye...

I KEEP WANTING TO LOOK
AT THAT MAN'S FAT ARSE

It's big and round
and a fly's just
landed on it.
I can't take my eyes
off that man's fat arse.
It doesn't interest me
in the slightest – not at all
but still I stare and my
girlfriend has noticed.
It's just moved a bit to
the right. I must stop this now...

IF YOU'RE NOT BUYING DON'T TOUCH

Arranged marriages
aren't so bad
one avoids the
selection, elimination
– wine tasting process.
I've been spat out
on several occasions...

FORTUNE TELLER

I don't need you
cried the old man
I'm eighty-four I know what
happened...

NO MORE REPRODUCTION

The first century was an experiment
The second was proof
The last eighteen sheer evil
only a nuclear war will
stop us sick bastards now...

NEGATIVE EXPERIENCE

Death makes every
single thing you
do in life absolutely
pointless...

RATS GETTING CLOSE

NECROPHOBIA

Ironically the only cure
for most people with a
fear of death is death
itself. My father was
one and died with a
stethoscope round his
neck – listening to his
last heartbeat.

KILLING TIME

It's ten-thirty in the morning
and I sit and wonder if anyone
in the world has been bitten
by a snake yet.

Now it's eleven – surely someone
must have severed an artery by now
or died in the operating theatre.

Now it's twelve and I'm late for
my psychiatrist.

THE CORLETTES

They were three blonde sisters
and I liked them all, especially
Janet, even though my friend said
she had a face like a parrot.
I found her purple hat in the street
once and brought it round to the
house – she wasn't very friendly
and when I asked her would she go
out with me immediately said no
and shut the door in my face.
I was heart-broken she was the
first girl I had fallen unsuccessfully
in love with – looking back I suppose
she didn't like my unfashionable
scruffy appearance, not to mention
my weird friends and eccentric father.
But going out with her would have
helped me enormously in those dark
days of my sister's schizophrenia and
mother's premature death. I saw her
cleaning her front door knocker when
I was last up in Liverpool. I had a
poem in the Guardian that day and
thought of going over and showing it
to her, but I don't suppose it would
have done any good, not now anyway.

DISAPPOINTING RESULT

First in Maths
second in French
best school project
  Became a peeping tom...

Captained a team
sang in the choir
butted a bully
  A peeping tom no less...

Trustworthy and smart
popular and punctual
conformed with ease
  A budding peeping tom...

Four A levels and
a university place
but no sign of a girl-friend
It's binoculars in the park
for our son
  He's a bleedin' peeping tom...

SHARED LETTER-BOX

Stealing people's mail
is fun to do
unless of course
they think it's you.

Money and chocolates
I've had them all
and none of them
addressed to Paul.

But be careful
when you play this game
in case your neighbours
do the same.

SOLITUDE

I live in my mind
  because I find
  peace of a kind
It's easy to do
when there's only you
  no kids or wife
  it's a quiet life.

TO DEFY HUMAN NATURE
JUST FOR ONE DAY

Fight it fight it
try your best to fight it
Smash it smash it
have a go at smashing it
Ignore it ignore it
see if you can ignore it
Forget it forget it
why not just forget it
and for twenty-four hours
don't be a slime bag...

BEING DEAD SUPERIOR

The living respect the dead
for they've done it – been
through it – suffered and
arrived, safe and sound.

RATS GETTING CLOSE

Candle-lit dinners, phoney chat
compliments and kisses
who needs that?

False sentiments, unreal affection
futile gestures cheap concern
Stuff your Valentine cards
Mustn't get attached to human trash.

In sickness and in health
my fuckin' arse
expect no sympathy if your
circumstances change
plenty more shit in the sea.

Snogging in parks sharing a bath
slowies, the flicks, fucking in
a friend's flat
I'd rather be a cockroach
than a lover.

Those who make contracts
are rewarded with brats,
mortgages H.P. debts
responsibility and misery.

I'd rather have a blackout
than an infatuation
lose a leg than have an affair
Sooner be a hermit than a couple.

EDINBURGH

If it wasn't for the cars
on the streets you wouldn't
know what century you were in.
As it is I keep thinking I'm
going to be shot by a musket,
challenged to a duel or waylaid
by footpads.

IS HE STRONG?

Funny the things you think
about on a first date – like
losing a fight at school –
failing one's exams – obscure
fears and phobias. Why is it
women bring out these feelings
in us? Is it because they're so
mercenary or so obsessed with
the continuation of the species?
Strength – strength – strength
she whispered in my ear – oh dear...

UNPLEASANT COMPANY

I had to ask him to stop
calling round in the end.
He kept treading in dog-dirt
and rubbing it into my carpet.
Once he brought a friend round
and he had stood in some too.
They both sat there smiling –
the living-room stank for days.

SWEET DREAMS

My dreams remind me of
how I saw things as a
young child – everything
a bit weird and strange –
new places, new people,
odd things happening –
but wonderful too.
My dreams remind me of
the never ending adventure
of childhood.

DEATH SENTENCE

This morning at about 11.30 my doctor
told me I had six months to live.
The man who had reassured me for so
long about everything from a lump on
the arm to a pain in the chest finally
told me I was going to die.
He acted no differently from when I'd
seen him on past visits – indeed he
might have been prescribing antibiotics
for some minor virus. I wasn't even sure
if he would mention it in passing to his
wife that evening – how he'd told a young
man of thirty-six he'd be dead by spring.
When I left his surgery I was surprised
to see everything was normal outside.
The world hadn't stopped to mourn my
predicament there was no minute's silence
observed, everyone carrying on as if
nothing had happened and I felt for the
first time in my life truly isolated
truly alone – absolutely bloody terrified.
I felt like shouting for help, screaming
about the doctor and the terrible things
he'd said to me. I wanted him arrested,
shot, strung up from a lamppost, nobody
talks to me like that. I thought of
waiting for him with a brick, but got
drunk in a bar instead...

PUBLIC HOUSES

Most boozers
are horrible places
full of losers
getting out of their faces.

Lounging on stools
letting the day slip by
talking with fools
whose only wish is to die.

They're a kind of home
albeit sad
for those all alone
and a little bit mad.

UNLIKELY POET

I told my sister I stuffed
a piece of fillet steak down
my trousers in the supermarket.
She said I bet Wordsworth wouldn't
have done that.

FOR YOUR THROAT'S SAKE
SMOKE CRAVEN A

I wish I could have been
a smoker before 1952 when
all the health scares started.
All that wonderful advertising –
doctors offering you one in the
surgery – smoking in cinemas on
buses and trains. No quitlines,
nicotine patches or warnings on
packets. No guilt worry or social
exclusion and costing much less too.
I wish I could have been a smoker
before 1952.

REPRESSED

He was so distressed when
he realised he was homosexual
he went to his local A and E.
An attractive nurse gave him
an injection of valium – he
tried to have a wank about her
when he got home.

BIG FRAUD

Have you noticed
middle-class women (often
wearing those ghastly red
ribbons) buying The Big Issue.
How they patronise the filthy
vendors and stroke their smelly
dogs – easing their wanky
consciences until the next
dire issue arrives...

NIGHTS

In memory of Philip Larkin

What are nights for?
nights are where we sleep
they come, time and time
over. They are to be happy
in. Where can we sleep but
nights?

Ah, solving that question
brings the dentist and the
milkman in their underpants
running down the street.

POSITIVE DISCRIMINATION

There's a little restaurant
in Chiswick where there's a
ban on courting couples and
the waiters are in wheelchairs;
the food is very good.

THE LONELINESS OF THE
LONG DISTANCE DRINKER

The drunk always stays
till the end – and leaves
with no money or memory
friends or dignity and
if he isn't barred will
not return anyway...

CANON KIRON

I was terrified of him,
though he didn't know
me from Adam, despite
announcing the death
of my mother at morning
assembly with a huge grin
on his face, and adding
snide remarks to my school
reports...

STRANGE

Where have all the
suicides gone?
why are they carrying on?
five thousand a year is
not enough so what is
going on?

Where have all the
suicides gone?
why are they hanging on?
five thousand a year is
a paltry sum just what
is going on?...

HAMPSTEAD HEATH

He was pushing sixty
obviously bonkers
asked me if I wanted
a game of conkers.

POEMS 2002–2003

JUST SHIT

People are tossers
become a hermit
and cut your losses.

COUNTING FOR MY LIFE

Sitting in my local pub
I find myself counting
the number of candles
on tables and imagine
they are the years I have
left to live. But seven
is not enough – so I stare
down at the floor and count
the number of discarded fag ends –
though nine is still too short –
so I turn my attention to the spirit
bottles behind the bar and with some
relief count fourteen – that's more like it.

TIME PASSES

I remember when I was eighteen,
still in flares with long hair
shocked that someone thought I
was twenty-nine, now I'm forty-one.

ENTERTAINMENT

News flash
loved ones
emergency services
emergency numbers
appeals
heroes
death-toll rising
extended news
Thoughts, condolences, sympathies –
who are you kidding –
everyone loves a good disaster.

WINSTON CHURCHILL PISSED

We'll fight them in the curry houses
We'll fight them in the pubs
We'll fight them in the toilets
We'll fight them in the sewers
We'll fight them in the launderette
We'll fight them in the job centre
We'll fight them in the betting shops
We'll fight them in the checkout queue
We'll fight them in the showers
We'll fight them in our beds
We'll fight them in our dressing-gowns
We'll fight them in our underpants
We'll fight them in the nude
We'll fight them in wheelchairs
We'll never surrender, but then again we might
probably.

WRONG SET-UP

I've been watching on TV
To Kill and Kill again.
But have decided I don't
have the right facilities
to become a serial killer –
not enough space for one thing,
and the walls are too thin –
not to mention nosey neighbours
and I don't really fancy a career
move at my age.

LONDON

It feels strange this second wave
of loneliness – more sad somehow.
I could handle it better in my twenties
when I was working and the city was still
relatively new, but not now – not at forty-two
a fat middle–aged man sitting alone in a bar
without leather jacket, looks, confidence or
enthusiasm. It must surely be time to go home
now – nobody will say I failed. Before I had
something to prove – more pride and the knowledge
that things would get better. But twenty years
is long enough I've done my penance, my time –
I'm going home.

THE RACE

Whenever the phone
rang in our house
my dad would make
a mad dash to get
there first – pushing
everyone aside and
shouting that he paid
the bill. He said it was
because he reacted to the
sound of a bell – but we all
knew he was a little unwell.

LAST MEAL

He had always enjoyed his food
so it was a hard decision what
to choose, and indeed he changed
his mind some twenty-five times
keeping the prison chef up all night.
He finally went for a traditional
English breakfast which he threw up
on his way to the death chamber.

SHOUTING ABOUT CANCER

How's your Cancer Birtill?
he shouted across the bar.
It's in remission I shouted back.
Oh good he roared, but do let me
know if you have Chemotherapy,
I'd like to know what it's like.
I will I shouted back.

BUT THEY MUST HAVE THEIR SPROGS

Life is a terrible trip
to lay on someone.
A struggle from start to finish
which does not diminish
but only gets worse
and then the hearse.

AT LAST

As soon as he lost
his fear of death
committed suicide

        promptly

ARTISTIC STATEMENT

Although he had paid for my book
and it was entirely up to him what
he did with it. I was still annoyed
when he started to bend the thing
while talking to me, so I told him to stop.
He responded by tearing the cover off
then folding it into four and stuffing
it in his back pocket.

ODD BEHAVIOUR

WATCHING THE BOX

It's not dying I so much mind
but everyone watching the box –
my box – staring, imagining –
recalling their own particular
moments with me, and me not being
able to communicate, rest or even
die with such a concentrated force
of eyes watching me. And at the burial
too – all eyes on me again – then the
wake – everyone talking about me and
in my flat – is there no peace?
No, I'll have to wait until they spout
that famous cliché life goes on, and
then forget about me.

ODD BEHAVIOUR

Just recently I've taken to putting
up two fingers at funeral cortèges,
and have been beaten up several times.
My Psychiatrist tells me it's just a
phase I'm going through – a kind of
mid-life crisis, not unusual for a
man of my age and background. I asked
him was it common, and he said in some
parts of India it occurs quite a lot
and referred me to the School of Tropical
Medicine.

FOUR TIMES A YEAR

It's always the same
Man drowns trying to save dog
Siege in East London
Travel chaos
Girl abducted
Just another Bank Holiday.

PERIOD

How strange to see Victorians
in old photographs in the prime
of life, walking around with
such confidence and self-assurance,
sometimes with their children,
who are also dead.

FIRST LOVE

Laughing bathing exercising
   clean underwear.

Checks his bank balance
tries for promotion
buys a jacket
washes his car.

Shows off, tells lies,
distrusts his mates,
thinks about his dead mother
kids, log fires, growing old together.

Stops getting drunk
goes to church
more exercises
more baths
Fresh jokes and confectionery.

Takes her to family home
shows her his old bedroom,
old toys, first school book,
Park where he played
hundreds of snaps and
   Mother's grave.

Strolls around the neighbourhood
holding her hand for all to see
What a find – an acquisition
Mine all mine aren't I clever.

Discovers she's a lesbian
never thought to ask
reverts to a four year old
Stamps his feet, yells
hits her, digs up his mother's
grave and sends her the bones.

SPOTTED

Drinking alone in my local pub
it's only when the upper deck
of a passing bus peer in at me
that I realize I'm having a shit time.

FAT MISOGYNIST

None of my mates ring me anymore
because they all have girl-friends.
If you can't beat them join them,
but I can't beat them and I certainly
can't join them.

FORTY-THREE

Yesterday I turned forty-three
and told a friend I'd outlived
Elvis Presley. He said I might
have outlived him in years,
but I certainly hadn't outlived him.
I went to bed early with a cup of cocoa.

SUMMER-TIME BLUES

It's here again, hot weather and flies,
long days, another football tournament
– how I hate it.

Picnics in the park, men with no shirts on
exposing sickly white skin – everyone wearing
stupid bright shorts.

Kids running amok in beer gardens,
fear of swallowing a wasp, pressure
to go on holiday – sweating like a pig.

Stinking tennis, noisy transistors,
weird things growing, not enough darkness
– talking shit at barbecues.

Laughing couples holding hands, old people
moaning, can't sleep at night and to round
it all off that three day nightmare –The
Notting Hill Carnival.

I don't think I can take another one of these
– let me die in March please.

GROTESQUE

All's fair in Love and War
I wonder what twat invented
                this Law.

PERFECT REVENGE

Although he was very experienced in First Aid
and knew the Heimlich Technique very well,
he still refused to perform the manoeuvre
when his old Headmaster began choking
on a piece of meat at their annual reunion
dinner.
He later explained to the Police that he quite
simply didn't like the guy – no charges were
brought.

TOO MANY HOURS IN THE DAY

What if the average time spent sleeping
was eighteen hours – people might be
less ill-tempered and happier – six hours
of life is quite enough, though not
much would get done I suspect – but who
cares.

THE PAST

I always prefer the past –
last year, last month,
last week, yesterday,
five minutes ago.
The past is a safer place
to be – to hang out in;
and you don't die.

WHY I NEVER WEAR
A RED POPPY

Men love to fight
Men like action
half of them lied
about their age to get in
and loved every moment of it –
best years of their lives –
the camaraderie, adventure,
heroic letters to their girls back home
not to mention the killing.
Men will always fight – in pubs
at football matches – beat up
their wives and children,
and that's why I never wear
a red poppy in November –
it just encourages them.

COURTING AT LAST

This morning I woke up to
the sound of heavy breathing
and thought that I'd finally
scored, but it was a dying pigeon
the cat had brought in.

BEHIND CLOSED DOORS

I've started a graffiti war in the toilet
of my local pub. It began innocently enough
with a short political statement, but now
it's turned quite unpleasant. Several people
appear to be involved judging by the different
handwriting and various threats have been made,
as well as an insulting drawing of myself depicting
me as a Snake. The Landlady has tried painting
it over a couple of times, but it just starts up again
with increasing nastiness. She's now thinking of
bringing the Police in, as the atmosphere in the pub
is quite tense.

THE BIG STINK

If only shit was pink
and smelt of roses –
I might be tempted to shag folk,
and I'd certainly enjoy my food more.

HARDLY WORTH THE TROUBLE

Hitler boasted of creating a thousand year Reich,
instead it only lasted twelve, one more year than
Margaret Thatcher. It wouldn't have sounded the
same at those mass rallies if he'd gone on about
a twelve year Reich, people wouldn't have been
impressed at all – they would have laughed,
and gone home.

2/8/12.15PM CAN YOU HELP?

The street is quiet again now,
the morbid onlookers have gone
about their business. The wreckage
cleared – the blood cleaned up –
the motorcyclist dead. A young
couple kiss near the tragic spot
unaware of the fatal accident which
occurred earlier. The icecream man
arrives, but no-one leaves their
house to buy one – it is a hot day
and he can't understand why. In
another part of the city a police
car moves slowly up the road of
the deceased man's parents.

PIGS LIVER

Last week I went to my first barbecue
and brought liver. The host was very angry
and said 'What kind of nut brings stinking
bloody liver to a barbecue?' 'A poor and
inexperienced one' I replied.

EMPATHY

He suddenly realized
what it was like to
feel like everyone else
and consequently felt like nobody.

FED UP

He committed suicide at four
hung himself from his bedroom door
couldn't take any more
done four.

TURN-OFF

I'd prefer to meddle
with an old car than
unfasten a woman's bra.

IN THE KINGDOM OF THE BLIND
THE ONE-EYED MAN RULES

The handsome young but hopeless
alcoholic goes out with the ageing
ex-beauty queen.
The academic professor with club foot
goes out with the uneducated teenage beauty with child.
The obese kind middle-aged man
goes out with the schizophrenic
with big tits.
The pathetic idiot with stutter
goes out with the dowdy bore
with demanding mother.
The rich gay pensioner
goes out with the criminal
athletic black man.
The up and coming young playwright
goes out with his ageing but helpful
literary agent.
The phoney mystic with personality
problems goes out with the impressionable
young drug addict.
The good looking but work shy dope
goes out with the manipulative career
woman and minds the kids.
Occasionally however some people
are lucky and manage to transcend
the barriers of social Darwinism
like the ugly and spotty working-class
labourer who marries the beautiful
daughter of a diplomat and inherits
a fortune.

PARANOID

He checked every new book
of poetry that came out
and every magazine to see
if anyone had stolen his poems.
He was obsessed with plagiarism,
then someone mentioned translations –
what about translations? and unable
to cope with the idea drove his
bubble car over a cliff.

SCARY

I remember as a child
being stung by a wasp
my father looked at his
watch and said I could
be dead within the hour.

I remember as a child
falling into some nettles
my father looked at his
watch and said I could
be dead within the hour.

I remember as a child
swallowing some bleach
my father looked at his
watch and said I could
be dead within the hour.

I remember as a child
having a temperature
of one hundred and three
my father looked at his
watch said he was a bit
slow but I'd probably
be dead within the hour.

BENEFIT KING

When I grow up I'm going to be
an astronaut a footballer a physicist
or be long term unemployed.

When I grow up I'm going to be
a rock star an actor a politician
or be long term unemployed.

When I grow up I'm going to be
a doctor a lawyer a fireman
or be long term unemployed.

When I grow up I'm going to be
an architect a marine biologist a painter
or be long term unemployed.

When I grow up I'm going to climb
Mt Everest invent things run my own business
or be long term unemployed.

When I grow up I'm going to have a beautiful wife
three lovely children a big house and flash car
or be long term unemployed.

NEAR LIFE EXPERIENCE

I stopped keeping a diary
it was getting embarrassing
I had nothing to write about
and somebody might have found it.

SPAN

Man born of Woman
has but a short time to live
but it's getting longer
          unfortunately.

WILLING TO CHANGE

EMBARRASSED FROM THE GRAVE

I'm so glad I've lived
for a reasonable period,
and now have some decent
dates for my headstone.
So that when people pass
by my grave and stare
don't think sadly how unfair.

SINGLE

Last Friday night I got chased
by celibate bashers in Camden Town.
They caught up with me outside the
tube station – called me an 'abstaining
bastard' and gave me one hell of a kicking.
The Police say it's a new type of 'hate crime'
which they haven't encountered before
but are taking very seriously.

FAN?

He said 'I was reading you
at three o'clock this
afternoon. I finished reading
you at a quarter past four,
and by five I had forgotten
about you. When is your next
book coming out?'

NIGHTMARE

Imagine waking up and discovering you were a fascist
having to ring all your friends and tell them you hate
blacks and jews – want to restore capital punishment
and send queers and gypsies to special camps.
Imagine waking up and realizing you were a fascist –
having to attend nasty meetings full of odious
characters, put racist stickers on lampposts and
give your local asian councillor abusive phone calls
in the middle of the night. Imagine it – feeling
bitter and twisted inside – what on earth would you do
if you really believed it? See your local doctor?
But he's a paki too.

A MEMORY OF LIVERPOOL

His name was Jimmy – horrible little man,
got cancer of the throat at forty-two
and survived – one of a very small group
I believe. He used to say the best
way of injuring someone in a pub
was to wait until they put a glass
to their lips and then give it a hard
shove. Even now when a stranger approaches
me in a bar I'm quick to remove the glass
from my mouth.

SOUR SIXTEEN

Face full of spots
Ma dying of cancer
Sister nutty as a
fruit-cake.
No job no girl no future,
and a list of neuroses
as long as your arm.
Must stay calm.

THE CARDIOLOGIST

'Man was made to work!' he bellowed
'Man was made to work! You've got
a thing about your heart and you're
only twenty. Get a job there's nothing
wrong with you – Man was made to work!'
He had two consultancies, NHS and private,
and dropped dead fell-walking in the Lake District
at forty-three – Man was made to work,
but perhaps not that hard.

THIRTY YEARS AGO

I wonder who lived in my flat
all those years ago when I was
so unhappy at grammar school –
suffering so badly. Some contented
old lady perhaps with a cat.
I can almost see her watering the plants
and taking an afternoon nap while
I struggled in double maths or
was being shouted at on the rugby pitch.

INSTIGATOR

I've had Quakers swing for me
and been burnt with a cigarette
by my local GP.

I've been head-butted by a blind man,
glassed by a nun, and wrestled to the ground
by my best friend's mum.

I've had the postman get me in a headlock,
the dentist pull my hair, and have been slashed
by a Spanish au pair.

I've been karate chopped by a Paramedic
kung fu kicked by a bin man, and driven
at by a Priest in a van.

I've been chased by Mongols
spat at by Stephen Hawking,
and bitten by an MP – and all just for talking.

The Criminal Injuries compensation
won't give me another penny,
the attacks have been so many.

WALTON

Growing up opposite
one of her Majesty's
prisons is not to be
recommended – the demented
screams in the middle
of the night. The sirens,
fires – prisoners on the
roof in protest. And our
local priest telling us
to say a prayer for the
last man to be hanged in
Britain one bleak Winter's
morning in 1964.

CAN'T PLAY THE FASCIST NO MORE

I used to like
to goose step
until I got sciatica,
now when I'm drunk I
have to make do with
a Roman salute
or click of the heels.

SUDDENLY

Suddenly I remembered
spelling the word suddenly
for the first time in my
thick lined exercise book.
I must have been seven and
added an extra e.

FLASHBACKS

My father seemed a little nervous
when I told him I could think back
as far as nineteen sixty-three,
and when I began recalling weird
incidents – immediately fitted
a yale lock on his bedroom door.
I wonder what for?

HUMAN CAUSES

Human causes
human causes
let's have no more
human causes.

Human causes
human causes
I'm so sick of
human causes.

Human causes
human causes
always end in
human corpses.

AT THE VET

'What's your cat's name?'
    'Tinker'

'What's his date of birth?'
    '2nd of April 98'

'What's his National Insurance number?'
    'What?'

'Has he ever been a member of a trade union?'
    'No'

'Has he ever been a member of the Communist Party?'
    'Not to my knowledge'.

TOO GOOD

I was putting the cat's
lunch out today – delicious
chunks of rabbit and liver
in a rich gravy. It looked
so nice I decided to eat it
myself and gave Tinker an
apple instead.

UGH!

Men are pathetic
Women are worse
Cats are best –
better than the rest.

WINTER

The cat slipped on the ice
and the birds in the trees
laughed their heads off
as did the mice.

EYE CONTACT

'Don't look at me if you're
not going to give me any money'
cried the beggar as I passed
him by. 'Don't look at me,
it ain't free.'

ON LEARNING OF A CLASS MATE'S DEATH
IN A ROAD ACCIDENT AT THE AGE OF NINE

Life's great,
but you can die!

AFTER THE PARTY

I got a taxi
He asked me did
I enjoy today
I said no
He asked me did
I enjoy the party
I said no
He asked me was
I enjoying the
ride home
I said not really
He asked me did I
think I would enjoy
tomorrow
I said it was most
unlikely
He asked me if I
lived on my own
I said don't we all
He asked me why I
was such a miserable git
I said just here will do fine.

THE VULTURE

Each Friday morning he'd take off to
attend a funeral, it didn't matter whose
it was, just as long as there were plenty
of sad faces and a large wooden box in view.

He'd put on his best clothes eat a full
breakfast and set off whistling down the
road, stopping at the local store for mints
and a paper.

He'd normally sit at the back of the church
as unobtrusive as possible soaking up the gloomy
atmosphere. He especially loved to see the
carrying of the coffin and the grieving
relatives behind.

Often he'd follow the procession to the
graveyard, observe the burial and pester
people for details. Occasionally he was
invited back by mistake for tea and sandwiches.
This of course was a special treat.

Then one day whilst hurrying to a funeral
he collapsed in the street and died. Nobody
rang for an ambulance, nobody did anything.
For weeks his body lay there decaying and
smelling, half eaten by dogs. Until one day
two men from the council came and set fire
to what was left of it. They put the bones
into a black bin-liner and flushed them down
the sewer.

ONE TO A HUNDRED

There's a number out
there waiting to claim you.
Somewhere between one and
a hundred it's out there waiting,
shocking but true, one of those
years is definitely for you.
One day in one calendar month
in one year will be yours –
your death day. One to a hundred
it waits for you.

SAVED BY A MISUNDERSTANDING

I always thought
sins of the flesh
meant not bathing
very often, consequently
few women sleep with me.

CAUGHT IN THE ACT

My wife plays backgammon with
two daft coalmen discusses
schizophrenia with the milkman
swaps stamps with a flirtatious
postman but she slept with my
best pal – twenty years down the
drain cos our relationship was
based on a sausage entering a
steak pudding – shame.

Talks politics with a cheeky
fellow from the prudential
confides in a neighbour with
a string of sex offences
sometimes arm-wrestles a hawker
called George – went and screwed
my boyhood pal – unforgivable.

Jogs with male models
sunbathes with squaddies
gave my dad a wank on his
death bed – did it with my
bezzy – twenty years up the
spout cos our friendship was
based on a sausage entering a
steak pudding – and I'm no better.

P.S All the walks by the sea no longer seem important –
thoughts of sweat and discarded underpants take over.

A DYING MAN'S THOUGHTS

Will I outlive this new extra large
bottle of sauce?
Will I outlive the giant box of tea bags
my sister brought round?
Will I outlive this mega tube of toothpaste
or the light bulb I've just fitted?
Should I buy this bottle of orange squash?
Will I be able to finish it? Or will it
outlive me?

CONFRONTATION

His horrible dog was not
on a lead so I stared at
him and then the dog.
He stared back I stared
at the dog the dog stared
at him he stared at the dog
and the dog stared at me.
We both stared at the dog
and it barked. 'That thing
should be on a lead' I said
'So should you' he replied.
'Don't talk rubbish I've
never bitten anybody.'

LUNCH WITH THE SICK

She kept pestering me
to take her for a meal.
So I took her to my local
hospital canteen – she walked
out in disgust, but I thought
the shepherds pie was rather good,
not to mention the rice pud.

AN ABOVE AVERAGE REVENGE

I didn't like the chap
so as he took his afternoon nap
I put a snake through his flap.

HOW LONG HAVE I GOT?

God I can't stand it anymore
I want to know my score.
How long have I got?
Have I had my lot?
All this suspense
Is making me tense.
I want to know my fate
I want to know the date.

THE MIDDLE-CLASSES AND SMOKING

They objected to me smoking a cigarette
outside a restaurant – yet told me they
had three cars. I don't drive myself,
and cars cause more pollution than
cigarette smoke. Also over a million
people a year are killed by cars
worldwide, but I've never heard of anyone
being run over by a packet of fags –
two-faced old bags.

USELESS POET

Never mind the muse
the man can't change a fuse.

THE METROPOLIS

I know it has a transient population.
But where does everyone go?
I'll be fucked if I know.

REJECTION

Went on a date
She turned up late
Said I'll be your mate
I was full of hate
Went home to masturbate.

HONOUR THY FATHER AND MOTHER

They held the new born baby
He said take it one day at a time.
She said every cloud has a silver lining.
He said we're all in the same boat.
She said positive thinking helps.
He said you might be lucky.
She said pack up your troubles.
He said there's a cure for most things these days.
She said it might never happen.
He said we're all in this shit together.
She said what's that lump on his head.
He said such is life, and the baby kept crying.

LUDDITE

I hate computers,
and use a typewriter instead,
although I think I'm the only
person that still buys tippex,
and I'm sure my newsagent thinks
I'm sniffing it, after seeing me
have a fit.

DENTISTS

What a horrible name
I'm sure they're insane.
They don't seek fame,
just fear and pain,
and you can't complain.

BAD TIMING

I said to the priest
'Father I'm so full
of hatred' – he burst
out crying and told
me he was dying.

LONDON TODAY

She talks glibly about
gruesome murders, road accidents
fires and the like – then smiles
and sez have a good weekend – this
can't be right.

RISE AND SHINE

It is dawn on Culloden Moor
I have just woken up exhausted
and hungry and realized that
I have to fight a bloody battle
very shortly. There are men of
all ages lying around me – many
will be dead or mutilated in a
few hours time – all these fine
bodies cut to pieces. I am tempted
to get up and walk away, but someone
would surely shoot me. The man next
to me has just woken – he winks at
me – 'fine day for a massacre' he says.

WARNING

My mother told me
never to accept food
from people with glasses,
quite right too – four-eyed
bastards – what do they know
about the joys of the palate?
Half of them can't even distinguish
between a herring and a roast chicken.

KIDS POEM

The sun is scum,
it follows me round
and burns my bum.

HURTFUL REPORT

It knocked me for six
it was from a woman
an attractive woman
– a woman I fancied.
It mentioned my appearance
and personal hygiene –
said I was suppressing
whatever abilities I might have.
I became withdrawn for the
rest of the term.

HANDICAPPED

You only go round once
and look what I've been
given to make the trip
with. I'll be lucky to
get half way.

SORRY

Trying to extract apologies
from some people, is like
trying to get blood from a stone.
They wriggle and squirm, as if
their very life depended on it.
Thank-yous however can be more
easily obtained.

LIVING DANGEROUSLY

I once met a man in a café
who said the life experience
was not in the slightest bit
dangerous – even the first world
war he exclaimed wasn't dangerous,
and he had a relative who survived
the titanic. He also said he never
watched the news or bought papers,
but I noticed he was carrying a knife,
and took an extra valium before going
to bed that evening, and slept peacefully
through the great storm of eighty-seven.

VILE

Nasty little people
watching nasty little soap operas
waiting for nasty little story lines
to develop – so they can justify their
nasty little lives.

INFIDELITY

Relationships
  founded
on another's
  hurt and pain
can never be very
  satisfying
although they often
  are
even after a suicide
they smugly carry
  on I'm told.

CITY OF NERVOUS TICKS

Once when I was bored in a pub
I blew up my crisp bag and popped it.
The guy next to me said quietly,
'Don't do that I'm from Belfast.'

SCREWS

There was a few of us
combing the ground with sticks –
looking for my brother's pipe
I had dropped earlier – quite
unaware we were outside the warders'
drinking club, until half a dozen of them
still in uniform rushed out and gave us
a hiding. 'They were looking for trouble'
I heard one say in a geordie accent.
It gave me a taste of what prison life
must be like, and I vowed never to go.
I was fourteen and lost a tooth.

SNAKES AND SEX

Snakes don't sleep around
snakes are very loyal.
In fact they keep the
same partner for life
and don't go in for this
casual bunking up at all.
And if you kill a snake
its partner will come
looking for you, and if
it catches you will give
you one hell of a bite.
I believe that's why people
bury them.

GLASGOW'S MILES BETTER

But stay there a while
and you'll eventually
get the Glasgow smile.

MOVE OR YOU'LL DIE

I don't want to die in London
they'll not bury me here.
I'm off to Glasgow, but then
I don't like their hospitals
so I'll move to Brighton or
maybe Wales – no I wouldn't
get an ambulance there –
nobody seems to die in Cornwall,
especially if they're passing
through. I could go abroad of course
only I wouldn't like a lot of foreign
nurses running around shouting:
It'll have to be Liverpool then but
I don't fancy some doctor I was
at school with diagnosing my special
and unique brand of cancer – so
I think I'll just keep moving around
and then perhaps I'll die on a train.

POET TO POET

Gerard, Gerard, Manley,
Hopkins, Hopkins.

Dung Rhythm.

Robert Heatwave

When two paths diverge,
take one and stop being
a stupid fuck.

William Wordsmith

I wander'd lonely as a poet
full of bullshit and didn't know it.

MAD

During my first psychotic episode
strangely I could understand T.S.Eliot,
but not John Hegley.

THE UNKNOWN POET

Think of all the unrecognised
poets before the 1890s when
illiteracy was common – all
that wasted talent. I wonder
how many gifted geniuses never
even got a chance to sign their
own name.

POETRY EVENING

It's always enjoyable
listening to John Heath-Stubbs.
He has such a strong personality.
He takes you back to a different time,
and you always get a glass of wine.

BOOK SALE

I said it's all free verse.
He said why are you charging
me a tenner then?

NOWT SO BORING AS FOLK

People are much of a muchness –
restricted by predictable human nature,
which they rarely rise above.
It's the same the world over,
once you've overcome the language
barriers and not so different cultures.
I once met a Buddhist – he smiled a lot,
and tried to get off with my bird,
                                        turd.

DYING INSTITUTION

I wish they'd leave pubs alone
if I wanted stupid armchairs
I'd stay at home.

And everywhere serving plates
of food to put you off the
drinking mood.

Fruit machines and quizzes
I can't stand – these irritations
should be banned.

Then there's women with their silly
drinks and noisy brats, and whatever
happened to beer mats?

Football constantly on the TV
it doesn't fucking interest me.

And soon you won't be able to smoke
the whole thing's becoming a joke.

I'll be forced to drink at home
and spend all night on the bloody phone.

FRIEND OR FOE?

Are we naturally horrible?
Is it just easier to be nice
to each other?
Is it all just an act?
Do we really want to kill
each other?
Mother, brother, lover,
and is this niceness
just a cover?
Friend or foe?
I'd like to know.

NO ONE KNOWS FUCK ALL!

Opinions, opinions,
I've got no opinions.
How can you have opinions?
Opinions are mixed – mixed-up
bloody opinions – hypocritical,
inconsistent lousy fuckin' opinions –
the curse of all us minions.

I WONDER

They like me
because I don't
like myself
I am not a threat,
I don't like myself
because I don't
like them, and
they are a threat.

FEAR

I went through a period
of shaking my head as a
child and once my dad
arrived home unexpectedly
and collected me from school
and it got worse so he beat
me and shouted and passers-by
looked on in dismay and someone
said I must be possessed and it
got so bad I couldn't stop and
I felt sick and dizzy and he
dragged me to the doctors and
said if I didn't stop they'd
lock me up in a home and I cried
and then stopped and have been
frightened ever since.

LET'S HEAR IT FOR THE MENTALLY ILL!

They don't push you around
or sleep with your wife.
They don't enter politics
or refuse you a smoke.
Let's hear it for the mentally ill!

They don't have big egos
or drive fast cars.
They don't go jogging
or play five a side.
Let's hear it for the mentally ill!

They don't travel abroad
or dress up smart.
They don't become famous
or compete in any way.
Let's hear it for the mentally ill!

They don't attend weddings
or have much fun.
They don't have children
or live that long.
Let's hear it for the mentally ill!

LEGS

My name's Bill Gough
and I've just had a leg cut off
  I'm not joking
it was caused by smoking.
It's too early to tell
if I'll lose the other one as well.
  What a bummer.
  Just before summer.

PSYCHOTIC EPISODE

They must have thought I was Martin Luther
reincarnated when I walked into the church
that evening, having not slept for five days,
and began knocking all the candles off the altar,
and decked the Abbot who tried to stop me.
Then later when three of them were restraining
me in the sacristy – calling them the Inquisition.
Well they were Dominicans, formerly the Black Friars,
and looked quite intimidating in their hooded robes.
The one I hit, like a good Christian visited me
in hospital the following week – he looked a bit uneasy
when I got up off my bed suddenly to light a cigarette.

A WEEK IS A LONG TIME IN DRINKING

Lost my job
Lost my wife
Lost my wallet
Lost my licence
Lost my sanity
and got my head kicked in.
When most people are ill they
get flowers, alcoholics get
black eyes.

TOO CLOSE TO CALL

Life's better than dust,
but only just.

THE VOLUNTARY EUTHANASIA SOCIETY

Exit listens
Exit's right
Exit helps
you day and night.

Exit care
for those who dare
Exit's a friend
right till the end.

Exit's free
for you and me
ring them today
It'll be okay.

TO WHOM IT MAY CONCERN

I apologize for my time
spent on this horrible earth,
and for my totally pointless
and unnecessary birth.

SUICIDE

One of the advantages of committing suicide
is that you can choose a relatively painless
and dignified death. Yet it often amazes me
the grotesque methods some people use,
like jumping in front of a tube train –
What's that all about? The traumatized driver
gets a week off work and the tubes are disrupted
for hours. Slashing one's wrists isn't much better –
what a bloody mess. I once knew someone who jumped
off a block of flats when all the kids were coming
home from school – he didn't die immediately.

NOT FICTION

Sydney Carton
was a very sick man,
tragic and misunderstood.
He needn't have thrown
his life away in order
to save face or gain grace.

GLASGOW 1990

Lord Haw-Haw
said 'we won't bomb Govan.
Govan will drink itself to death'.
But ironically it was there I went
to my first AA meeting – funny place
to get sober.

TRIPPING ON LIFE

Get into it
not out of it.
Animals seem
perfectly happy
and so were you
in your nappy.

CRYPTIC

Faith is like a crossword puzzle.
The clues are there, but you have
to work out the answers for yourself,
and discover where everything fits.

CAPITALISM?

Only a sinner
can be a winner
in this sick old
world of ours.

DO NOT DISTURB

DO NOT DISTURB

If I'd been asleep for a thousand years
and some fool happy couple offered me birth,
and the chance to come back to sad planet earth.

I'd tell them no thanks because I've been there
before – seen what it's like, and don't want
anymore.

Their politics, religion, and evil wars,
the suffering, misery, and unfair laws –
needing drugs and alcohol just to get through.
I don't want another go and be honest, do you?

TAXI RIDE

My mother was having an angina attack,
so my dad suggested we get a cab, even
though we were only going up the hill.
The driver got very angry – said he'd
been queuing at the rank for an hour
hoping for a big fare. My dad told him
he was a servant of the general public,
and to 'Shut-up!'. He continued to curse us
under his breath, while my mother looked sad,
and placed a small white pill on her tongue.

A BOY'S BEST FRIEND IS HIS MOTHER

He was only six when she threw
him from the balcony of their
twelfth storey home. He must
have felt heartbroken flying
through the air, knowing his
Mummy didn't care – definitely
no love lost there.

HOPELESS

Lonely, bored, depressed,
three in the afternoon
and still not dressed.

HUMILIATED

He killed both his parents
and his sister, as well as
a neighbour and the local priest.
Sentenced to life in prison – in
his first year he killed a fellow
inmate and a guard. The subject of
a television documentary some years
later, when asked by the interviewer
what he would do if he was released.
He said he'd 'kill more humans'.
His Psychiatrist attributed much of
his behaviour to an incident which
occurred when he was at Primary School,
when a female class-mate beat him in
a playground fight and sat on his face.
He went berserk afterwards smashing windows
and assaulting staff.

MID-LIFE CRISIS

'But doctor, look at my hands,
Just look at them, they're all wrinkled'.
'Well, you're nearly fifty. What do you expect?'
was the unsympathetic reply.
'But I haven't lived! I haven't bloody lived!'
he exclaimed, tears rolling down his face.
'Well, that's not my fault. Would you like
a prescription for some hand cream or perhaps
an anti-depressant?'

9/11

He'd been unhappy for a long time,
and had been planning his suicide
for months. So he was the first
to jump from The World Trade Centre
that day, even before the fire had
taken hold. A short note was found
on his body – it read 'This suicide
is entirely my own fault, no-one else
is to blame at all.'

UNSETTLING

I've noticed my Psychiatrist
has a number of strange tattoos
on his arm – HATE, BLOOD and HONOUR,
and I can't quite make out the other one,
but I think it sez KILL ALL QUEERS,
as if I haven't got enough fears.

BREATHING IS WRONG

Breathing is unnatural
Breathing is absurd –
One should try not to do it,
resist it, stop it – hold it
for as long as you can, and
put a plastic bag over your head.
You'll enjoy it more, being dead.

POETRY PLEASE?

I told him I had a new book
of poetry out and asked him
if he wanted to buy a copy –
only a fiver? As I didn't
have it on me I offered to
leave it behind the bar for him
if he gave me the money up front,
I was a bit short. He seemed a little
indecisive, so I offered to send it to him
in the post. He paused for a moment then
handed me a fiver and said 'Keep the book' –
His friend looked embarrassed.

IN MY OPINION

The entire nation
should practice flagellation.
A befitting penance for our wicked ways,
and we'd all feel the benefits in just a few days.

HAVE YOU HEARD?

Every time you meet him
he tells you someone's dying,
but it's never true he's always lying –
He's had people crying, but I've told him
I'm not buying.

NOVEMBER 22ND LONDON

It never really got light today,
I've seen days like it before
this time of year. But the leaves
they are so beautiful this autumn,
such unusual colours; We should be
grateful to the Victorians, strange
though they were, for planting so many
trees, it must have taken their minds
off sex – poor souls.

GLOBAL WARMING

It was snowing when I woke
this morning and was sunny
at midday. There was a party
having their Christmas dinner
in the pub and I got stung by
a bloody great bee – All this
in mid-February. I've also
noticed those old guys with
'THE END IS NIGH' signboards
seem a lot more confident
these days – have a certain
spring in their step.

STEAK

My parents were quite poor,
and I remember they both looked
a bit sad, when at the age of ten
I told them I'd never tasted steak.
'You will do when you grow up and
get a job' my father said. But I
never grew up or got a job, and now
I'm forty six and I still haven't
tasted bloody steak – what's it like
for Christ sake?

ALCOHOLIC

I often talk to strangers in bars,
and sometimes wonder what it would
be like to meet my late parents –
out for a drink together in their
early courting days. Would I bore
them too? Ruin their evening perhaps?
I can almost hear them saying – 'What
a sad lonely man' as they hurriedly leave,
though I prefer to think of them as being
polite and kind.

SWALLOWING THINGS

I'm always swallowing things in my sleep,
I wake up choking, thinking I have minutes to live.
Normally it's small items like pens, nails,
cigarette lighters, but on one occasion I
managed to swallow my glasses case, and was
about to dial 999 when I came to my senses.
My doctor says it's just anxiety and to keep
a glass of water by my bedside, but I'm frightened
I'll swallow the glass.

PSYCHIATRIC WARD

I enter the TV lounge with usual apprehension
and sit next to an attractive new arrival
I tell her I like her dress, she looks away
in disgust and mutters something about
sticking a pen in my eye. I get a cold feeling
in my stomach and change seats. 'The Terminator'
is on TV and although people stare in that direction,
nobody is really watching it. Then one patient
gets up suddenly and pushes the television over.
Somebody shouts and a brief argument ensues,
but the set is broken – terminated! Everyone
carries on staring at the vacant space.
A big lady in a pink dressing-gown and one slipper
starts laughing – she calls us all devil worshippers
and leaves the smoke filled room. I smell food,
it's nearly lunch-time and I'm starving, a side effect
of the medication. I've put on half a stone since I've
been here. Then the alarm goes off (Third time today)
Nurses run to guard the exit. I haven't got enough
cigarettes.

MISTER CORCRAN

His was the first corpse I ever saw –
washing his car one Sunday morning
in 1970, he collapsed – they said
he was dead before he hit the ground,
heart failure. A few people tried to
revive him, but he just lay there.
I watched on my bicycle in astonishment –
he wasn't that old. I remember he wore
a ragged green pullover quite visible
through the crowd, and baggy jeans.
I knew his son from school – who
returning home from mass with his sister
a little later, after the ambulance had gone,
seemed to sense immediately that something
wasn't right in the street, and he went pale
and looked scared. He was never the same after
that, something left him that day and never
returned – Even in his twenties when I last
saw him, the sadness and loss of that Sunday
morning was still there.

MINESWEEPING

I remember the first drink I stole
in a pub – it was in The Big House
on Lime Street – they were a posh couple
from the South. He went to get something
from his car and I lifted his cool fresh
pint of Skol lager in a tall chilled glass.
I watched him return, he looked shocked.
'Somebody's stolen my drink!' he said
to his girlfriend – 'What kind of a place
is this?' he exclaimed. 'What kind of a place
is it for Christ sake?' He ordered a short
and began looking at people suspiciously,
his girlfriend was smiling.

NINETY-TWO IS THE NEW EIGHTEEN

Some deluded and pathetic middle-class
lovers of life are beginning to say
that seventy is the new fifty, it's
not true of course, they are really
very old and are going to die quite soon,
some of them in a lot of pain.

DISILLUSIONED POET

I'm organising a book burning
bonfire next summer at Hay-on-Wye,
for all the poetry no-one wants to buy.

CHRISTMAS WITHOUT MUM

It just wasn't the same
that first Christmas after
her death, everyone felt it
as we ate our dinner totally
subdued and cheerless.
It was the same the year after –
a sombre and slightly embarrassing affair;
Until one by one we stopped coming home,
and my dad went to his sister's in Yorkshire.

HANDS OUT YOUR POCKETS!

That's all he ever said our old Headmaster.
You could hear him shouting it all over the school.
It stayed with me though – probably the only useful
thing I learnt at that place; after all if you trip
in the street and your hands aren't free, you could
do yourself a lot of damage. I often wonder if this
is why he said it, to protect us from serious injury,
or did he just think it looked slovenly? It was
all right for him though, being a priest he wore a
cassock which didn't have any bloody pockets.
Maybe he wanted some?

OLD BAG

This old woman
started talking to me in a bar,
she must have been nice looking
when she was young, so I said
'Why talk to me now and not forty
years ago when you were a beautiful
young woman?' 'You might have harassed
me then' she replied with a nervous smile.
'Well I'm ignoring you now' I said, and
carried on reading my paper.

THE TRUNK

My elder sister bought it for college
in the mid-seventies. She had intended
to become a Primary School teacher, but
suffered a serious break-down during her
first term and came home. All she had ever
wanted was to go away to college, and it
was heart-breaking to see her so ill and
demoralized. She planned to go back the
following year, and regularly added things
to the trunk, and proudly kept her student
I.D. card and other college artefacts in her
wallet; but she never did go back and the large
heavy trunk just lay there, taking up space
in her small bedroom, until finally after
a couple of years, when her condition didn't
really improve and it was obvious she would
never return to study, my father told her
to get rid of it. I remember she had tears
in her eyes the day it went.

GEOFFREY MILLER

The Landlord's name over the door
said Geoffrey Miller licensed to sell
beer, wines and intoxicating spirits –
so in we went. 'Are you Geoffrey Miller?'
I said to a bald fat man with a small
moustache 'Yes' he replied 'Would that
be the same Geoffrey Miller licensed
to sell beer, wines and intoxicating spirits?'
'It is indeed' he said looking slightly proud
of himself. 'Right we'll have some of that'
I said and we both sat down, and for several
hours consumed everything Geoffrey Miller
could throw at us. Finally I fell off my stool,
and my friend threw up on the bar, at which point
Geoffrey Miller turned nasty and refused to sell us
any more of his beer, wines, or intoxicating liquor,
and threatened to call the Police if we didn't leave.
So we said 'Fuck You Geoffrey Miller!' and left.

THE COLONEL'S BLOOD-BATH

Call me chicken if you like,
but I wouldn't go to a KFC
take away after the pubs close
of a weekend – there's nearly
always a punch-up or a stabbing.
Some very angry young men use those
places – frustrated and disappointed
they haven't scored in the pub with
the woman of their dreams, they try
to console themselves with a two piece
dinner and beans, but it's never enough
and not even the fillet zinger burger
stops them getting vicious and rough;
Finger lickin' good it may be, but I wanna
keep mine and my teeth, and I don't want
Colonel Saunders sending me a wreath.

HELL ON EARTH

I don't think any First World War poet
would have bothered with a creative
writing course. They learnt their skills
in the trenches ankle-deep in sludge, and
bled their hearts out in No-Man's Land.
No-one could teach them how to write,
they were there – saw everything; what else
could they do but write, or go mad?

SHITE

In the beginning there was shite
followed by more shite
followed by even more shite
until there was just shite

SMASH POSITIVE THINKING!

Smash positive thinking
show it up for the filthy cheap
lie that it is.
It's this filth – this wicked
con – this vile perverted form
of self-deceit that has kept
this foul planet with its
depraved wretched souls in
a confused state of optimistic
misery and torture for over
two thousand years.
Smash positive stinking thinking
for it and it alone is the cause
of our continuous suffering,
our hopeless and most unsatisfactory
existence. Smash it now, this minute.
Refuse to think positively. After all
why should you have to?

AID THEM NOT

Don't get involved with
First Aid. It's depressing
and horrible and you don't get paid.

So let them bleed
and let them choke
bloody awful human folk.

And watch them squealing
as they burn, it really
isn't your concern.

CHANGING WORLD

People are living longer too.
Those you wish would vanish
no longer do.

NEW POEMS

AUSTRALIA

Men are men
twelve thousand miles away
in the land of skin cancer.

Big burly and burnt
swatting flies swigging schooners
bonking brown sheilas.

Raucous toughies
forthright and sporty
taking it easy in a land
of desert and bush.

Not a whiff of culture
from this backward colony
on the edge of civilisation
A raging inferno peopled
by bird-brains.

As historic as Milton Keynes
a nothing place offering only
heat to moronic sunbathers
with stagnant minds.
A cheap version of America
without the interesting bits.

Flying around the world
the youth of this unsatisfied nation
search for roots answers and inspiration.

But why should generations
have to pay for the crimes
of their lumpen ancestors
living in total exile in a barren wilderness.

Isn't it time to forgive, forget
and rehabilitate this forgotten
race of reactionary tarzans
suffering in purgatory –
don't put a shrimp on the barbie for me.

RUDOLF HESS

Big healthy Hess gone to his God –
fine strapping Nazi of a man up there
with his merciful maker, still blathering
on about Jews. The lonely, lanky flyer of
Messerschmitts in the middle of the night,
boring everyone with his anti-semitism –
still unbalanced and missing Hitler terribly –
saying how he'd like to live in a castle in
Scotland, go salmon fishing and play golf.

AT THE DOCTORS

Do you smoke?
Not now thanks doctor.
I'm not offering you one, stupid.
How many do you smoke a day?
Three.
That's not bad.
Three packets.
Oh that's far too much. Why don't you switch
to a pipe?
Why don't you?
But I don't smoke.
I've only got your word for that doctor.

STEALING FROM MY MOTHER'S PURSE

She never had much,
but I stole anyway –
anything from a shilling
to a ten bob note – It left
her short, I know it did,
and sometimes I felt bad.
She would hide her bag in
the most ingenious places,
but I always found it, and
went out to buy sweets and
cigarettes, knowing there would
be no milk in the fridge that day.
Once I stole a pound and she told
my elder brother who threatened me
with a knife – I had to give it back.
It saddens me that she died before I
was old enough to work, and give her
something towards the housekeeping –
repay all the money I stole.

SMELLY UNDERPANTS

The housekeeper at the writers' retreat
seemed to like me at first, but then went
a bit cold. I think she peeped into my bag,
and realized I had no change of underpants
for the entire trip.

MY CLOSE SHAVE WITH CANCER

I met him outside the hospital
crying in his pyjamas. 'I've got cancer,'
he said – 'fuckin' cancer! Would you believe it –
Me! Who's never smoked a cigarette in his life!
Six months to live – fuckin' lung cancer.
You should have it the way you smoke, not me –
Why don't you have fuckin' cancer!'. I told him
I was very sorry; at which point he turned nasty.
'It's all your fault' he said. 'Chain-smoking in the
pub all the time – you gave me the fuckin' cancer!'
'Now hold on' I said. 'You can't blame me for your
filthy stinking cancer.' 'Oh yes I can' he roared,
and began strangling me; but I managed to break
free and ran away – My close shave with cancer.

LOURDES

He would go each year
and queue at the grotto
with the other incurables,
but would inevitably hobble
away disappointed with the
same bad leg – saying to himself
there's always next year – a miracle
is due, and it could be you.

JUDAS

We were returning from the Vet,
when we were approached by the local yobs.
They began making fun at my father – jeering
and giving Heil Hitler salutes because of his
moustache. I felt ashamed and self-concious,
and longed to be with the other boys. We walked
on quickly but as we turned the corner one of them
crept up behind him and grabbed his hat. I saw him
do this, but failed to warn my father who said later
at home I had betrayed him.

HEARTBEAT

Last night I lay awake in bed
listening to my heartbeat, it was
louder than normal and sounded strong
with perfect rhythm, and I felt sad –
sad that I was such a heavy smoker,
and generally abused myself – poor thing
I don't give it a chance.

THE SMELL OF THE SHIT

I remember as a boy being on a train
with my mother and this elderly well-dressed
man opposite kept repeating the words – 'The
smell of the shit', he kept saying it in an
aggressive tone. My mother thought he was
disgusting, but I thought he was quite funny.
I couldn't smell the shit then, but I can smell
it now – Oh yes, 'The smell of the shit, the smell
of the shit!'

GRAND NATIONAL DAY

I met him in the street,
and asked him if he was putting a bet on.
'No I can't' he said, 'I'm a vegetarian'.
What's that got to do with it I thought –
people have always got to be something.
I remember the year the IRA disrupted
the race, and the horses watched while
all the people ran.

TOILET

It was the only room in the house
that had a lock, so I would run there
for protection when I was in trouble –
a kind of sanctuary. Once after I had
arranged my dad's deck-chair so it would
collapse when he sat down I ran there.
My father said he would remove the door
if I didn't open it – I thought he was
bluffing, but off he went to get his tools,
then removed the door, and flushed my head
down the toilet.

TAKE ME OFF!

Most people that commit suicide
really only want to go to sleep
for a month or two – take some
time out, but alas it is not possible.
It's like being in a football match
that lasts eighty years – crying out
for a substitute to take over and give
you a rest.

SUICIDE ATTEMPT

There's nothing worse than a failed
suicide attempt – a damaged body,
and a spell on a Psychiatric ward.
So if you plan to take your own life,
be sure to do some research before you try,
if your intention really is to die.

THE WINDOW CLEANER

There was always a tremendous rush
to draw the curtains in the bedroom
whenever the window-cleaner came,
but he was often too fast for us,
racing up his ladder singing, and
catching my mum in her nighty having
toast and tea in bed. He would always
give a big smile and wave – My mother
hated him.

METALWORK

I couldn't hear him for one thing,
much less understand what he said.
But every Friday afternoon for an
hour I would suffer the torture of
a metalwork lesson. 'Everyone round
the bench' he would say and explain
our boring task for the afternoon,
but I was always left bewildered
and confused – standing there with
a piece of metal in my hand wondering
how I was going to convert it into a
shoehorn or some other such object.
'You have no interest in this subject
do you?' said Mister Smith one afternoon,
'no interest at all. You won't be much use
round the house when you get married.'

FIFTIES

My dad finally came home from his travels
when he was fifty – Home to an unhappy marriage
with six kids who didn't like him very much.
I don't recall him having any friends either,
nor did he drink or smoke, and he hated his job
at The City Analysts, where he was bypassed for
promotion in favour of younger men. He used to
get up very early when no-one was around, and
pretend to go to sleep on the sofa each night
after tea. Even at the age of seven I could tell
he was unhappy – It was as if it was all over for him.
I think it must have been his worst decade – He died
at seventy-three.

IT IS AGAINST THE LAW
TO SMOKE IN THESE PREMISES

It's degrading to have to go outside pubs
to smoke, and people nick your seat, and
sometimes your drink. It reminds me of the
1930's when men couldn't afford to drink,
so would congregate around pubs smoking.
It's a law against working-class people
in my opinion, and unlike the Fox-hunting ban,
we have bowed down and accepted it.

KILLER

I once read somewhere that Errol Flynn
killed a fellow schoolboy when he was
sixteen in a playground fight. I wonder
how the boy's mother must have felt when
Errol became a Hollywood star, and his face
was plastered all over the screen – big action
adventure hero, slaying dozens in sword fights.
Would she have been pleased by his early demise?
drinking himself to death at fifty.

CARDINAL HEENAN

My parents were both devout Catholics,
and when their marriage was in difficulty,
had an audience with Cardinal Heenan, then
Archbishop of Liverpool. He suggested they
had another child, despite the fact my mother
was forty-five; and in the same year he founded
the Grammar school I was to spend five long
miserable years at. It was as if he was planning
my life for me, and I used to curse him walking
along the school corridors, depressed – Wishing
I hadn't been born.

HAPLESS DAN

He used to describe himself
as a 'Family Man' until he
killed them all when he crashed his van.
Now he's just a man – a broken man,
a broken ex-family man, with a lifetime
ban.

STRANGE CONVERSATION

He was telling me about his holiday
in Paris – how he stayed in a friend's flat.
'I prefer it to hotels' he said. 'You can
wander round in your knickers in the morning.'
'In your knickers?' I said. 'Yes in my knickers.'
'I have to go' I said.

IN THE PUB

He accused me of listening
in on his conversation, and
told me to apologize to his
girlfriend, so I did, just
as Coward of the County came
on the juke box.

SOME SANTA

I finally realized Santa Claus
didn't exist when my dad tripped
over and fell onto my bed one Christmas.
I called him a fat slob, and he punched
me in the face.

FAST FORWARD

I can easily think back to thirty
years ago – can remember clearly
things that happened and how I felt,
but now at forty-eight when I try to
think ahead another thirty years –
fast forward, it's just darkness I see,
darkness and total oblivion, and I am
reminded of how brief our time is here.

HOUSE KEY

I came across it when I was last home
on a visit, and remembered how I used
to fumble around with it as a drunken
teenager, and how on some occasions
if it was very late my dad would put
the bolt on the door, and I'd have to
ring the bell and wake the house up –
there was nearly always a row.

LLANDUDNO REVISITED

I was last there forty years ago
on a family holiday, and passed
the council estate where we stayed
on the way in. My mother hated it,
and complained endlessly, but I thought
it was quite nice, and I think it was all
my father could afford – there was seven of us.
I remember I got lost on that holiday, and the
look on my father's face when I was found –
a mixture of love and fear. I think about it often.

ARNOLD HEAD

He was my Clinical Psychologist
for the best part of a year when
I was twenty – GP referral.
I mostly talked about my childhood,
but he wasn't very interested –
seemed to think I wasn't a serious case.
Once he fell asleep when I was recounting
a particularly traumatic incident –
even started snoring. His last advice
to me was to get myself a girlfriend.
'It will take your mind off things'
he said, chewing peanuts.

ALSO BY PAUL BIRTILL FROM HEARING EYE

Terrifying Ordeal
ISBN: 1870841 55 7   1998   £6.50

So Far So Bad
ISBN: 1870841 67 0   2000   £6.50

Rats Getting Close
ISBN: 1870841 78 6   2001   £4.50

Collected Poems: 1987–2003
ISBN: 1870841 91 3   2003   £10.99

Odd Behaviour (pamphlet)
ISBN: 1870841 51 4   2005   £3.50

Willing to Change
ISBN: 1905082 25 8   2006   £7.50

Do Not Disturb (pamphlet)
ISBN: 1905082 37 7   2007   £3.50

(price includes P&P to UK only)

For information about forthcoming publications, or our catalogue
of books (1987-2003), please send an SSAE. All orders are
attended to by return of post. You may also like to see our new
website where you can order all our books online.

Hearing Eye,
Box 1, 99 Torriano Avenue, London, NW5 2RX.

email: books@hearingeye.org
www.hearingeye.org